NO MORE TEST ANXIETY

Effective Steps for Taking Tests and Achieving Better Grades

© 1996 **Ed Newman, Ph.D.**

Published by Learning Skills Publications, LLC.
P.O. Box 642442
Los Angeles, CA 90064-2442

First Printing, September 1996

Library of Congress Catalog No. 95-078584

Newman, Ed, 1936-
    No More Test Anxiety
    Includes bibliographical references
    ISBN 0-9650930-0-x

Printed in the United States of America

Clip-Art Illustrations by T-Maker, Inc.

Dedicated to Sara

No More Test Anxiety

ACKNOWLEDGEMENTS

A number of talented people contributed their time and energy to NO MORE TEST ANXIETY. Annette Baran freely gave interest, support and ideas. Sara Berman offered many helpful suggestions, clarifying questions, and inspiration. Charles Britton made the first draft worth looking at a second time. Lori Milken used her sharp vision to spot the typos and missed punctuation. Clifford Nefsky offered valuable thoughts and honest opinions. Deborah Orlik used a sharp pen that helped the book immeasurably. Gary Panas brought his considerable skills to the cover and label designs.

My thanks to each of them. They made the job more doable and considerably easier. Without their contributions, this book would not be.

CONTENTS

GETTING THE MOST FROM THIS BOOK

Jeff is a pre-med student at a large university. He faced an important exam during his final year. Jeff needed to do well and allowed plenty of time to study and prepare. He began to feel anxious as thoughts of the exam filled his mind and the test date grew closer. Jeff grew increasingly concerned. The test assumed ever greater importance. Jeff found it more difficult to keep his mind focused. Studying quickly became an exhausting effort.

Jeff's focus and concentration began to fall apart. The material wouldn't "stick" in his mind. He tried harder, convinced that added effort would make everything right. But, the more he studied, the more he worried. By test time, Jeff was exhausted, anxious, and apprehensive. The only clear thoughts going around and around in his head were, "I know I'm going to blow it. I can't possibly succeed. I am a failure."

Shiela is a high school senior; she has taken the SAT three times. The last time she took the SAT, Shiela thought she was completely prepared. She had taken a prep course and done well on the practice exams. Going into the test she even had her bottled water and an assortment of snacks. Shiela felt apprehensive, but ready.

As the test began, Shiela felt more anxious than she would have liked. The first question she couldn't answer pushed her anxiety up a notch or two. The next question she didn't know made her panic. At that moment Shiela's thinking slowed down. She began to get an old, familiar ache in her stomach. From then on, it was all down hill. Uncontrolled anxiety had done Shiela in, again.

What It's All About

NO MORE TEST ANXIETY addresses the jitters, panic, knocking knees and sweaty palms you and tens-of-thousands like you suffer when it's time to study for, or take an exam. Those terrible sensations are your body's way of saying you've become "uptight" and "stressed out." A test is staring you in the face and you've suddenly lost control. The mind-numbing, heart throbbing discomfort is what keeps you from thinking clearly and doing your best. What you've got is all too common. It's called test anxiety.

Test-taking horror stories abound. They occur daily in every school, college, and university throughout this country and in other countries as well. Test anxiety occurs whenever a student is under excessive pressure to succeed and do well. Demands and expectations beyond the student's coping ability become overwhelming. The student feels helpless to change anything.

Most students, on occasion, will feel overwhelmed and anxious by the prospect of a test. Fortunately, they don't experience the anxious feelings all the time. For others, test anxiety is constant, and definitely interferes with their ability to get good grades.

Putting You Back in Charge

The problem is more than simply a case of worrying about an upcoming exam. It is quite natural for you to be nervous before an important test. In fact, numerous studies have shown that some anxiety is a definite asset. The heightened arousal that comes with a little anxiety can actually increase your energy and sharpen your thinking. However, the same studies found that more is definitely not better! Too much anxiety leads to a rapid decrease in your ability to think and concentrate. If you are test anxious, you know what it's like to endure weak performances and poor grades.

The focus of NO MORE TEST ANXIETY is to put you back in charge during tests. Chapter by chapter, you'll find proven ways to make studying and test-taking easier and more effective. You'll discover methods to help you overcome excess anxiety and feel more comfortable and at ease. The techniques described in the following chapters can be used when you are studying for an exam, or in the midst of taking one. They are effective for anyone preparing for a test, written or oral. Whether you are a student in high school or college, preparing for graduate school entrance exams, or facing licensing or employment exams, this book will help you to study better and take tests more successfully.

In seven steps, you'll learn how to achieve calm, confidence, and concentration. Step-by-step instructions will make it easy for you to become attuned to your own physical, mental, and emotional resources. You will clearly identify the ways you react to tests and examinations, and learn about the subtle levels of tension and stress that build within your mind and body. You'll learn to quickly release excess tension before it interferes with your thinking. You will find yourself back in control during stressful situations.

■ The first chapter, YOU AND ANXIETY, explains what test anxiety is all about. You'll discover how it affects you personally, and how it can impact your thinking and studying before a test. As you progress through the examples and techniques in each chapter and become aware of your own responses, you'll be developing your own anxiety and stress reduction program.

■ Step One: STARTING AT THE BEGINNING, addresses breathing, the foundation for virtually all relaxation strategies. Breathing is basic to reducing test anxiety and improving focus and concentration. By itself, deep and rhythmical breathing can reduce stress and bring a sense of calm and well-being. Knowing you can calm yourself anytime you want to is a big part of feeling in control.

■ Step Two: LETTING GO OF WHAT YOU DON'T NEED, introduces the world of physical relaxation. Eliminating tension via muscle relaxation is the second step in your program. From active progressive relaxation to passive visualization, each exercise focuses on body awareness. You'll learn a number of different ways of initiating a relaxation response. When you have finished Step Two, both your body and mind will know how it feels to be truly relaxed.

■ Visualization is the focus of Step Three: SEEING WITH YOUR MIND'S EYE. The ability to visualize can enhance learning and memory. You will learn that what you experience in your mind's eye gets reflected in your body. You'll find which of the five physical senses are easiest for you to visualize. And, you'll discover how to create and use visualizations for studying and taking tests.

■ Step Four: IMPROVING FOCUS AND CONCENTRATION, describes different techniques for achieving a deeply focused state of mind. Test anxiety leads to scattered, unfocused thinking that interferes with concentration. Auto-hypnosis is a simple way to quickly focus your thoughts toward a specific topic or goal. You will learn to create a protected inner place in your mind. Then, you can study and take tests without fear and anxiety.

■ Step Five: SEEING THE WORLD A DIFFERENT WAY, illustrates a number of exciting ways to change a negative attitude into a positive outlook. The anticipation of failure will change to an expectation of success. One of the major factors facing test anxious students is the belief that no matter how much effort they spend studying and preparing, the end result will still be failure.

Almost by definition, negative attitudes are self-defeating. A positive attitude is essential for a firm belief in yourself and your abilities. The truth is, you really don't know what special skills and talents lie within you. You have potential that is waiting to be discovered and expressed.

■ Step Six: IMPROVING THE ODDS, offers new techniques for studying, learning, remembering and recalling what you need to know for an exam. NO MORE TEST ANXIETY begins by focusing on relaxation. However, relaxation alone will not raise your test scores. You can be the most relaxed test-taker in the world, but if you don't know the material you'll simply be a wonderfully relaxed failure. You must know the information, and that means good study habits are absolutely essential.

■ Step Seven: TEST WISENESS, includes many proven, test-taking techniques. It explains the best ways to approach different kinds of classroom exams and standardized tests. Learning the material is of major importance. Demonstrating a command of the information during a test is equally vital. You have to be test-wise, which means knowing how to take tests successfully.

■ The last chapter, PUTTING IT ALL TOGETHER, shows you how to make it all work. You'll combine a positive attitude with relaxation, clear focus and concentration, effective studying techniques, and a knowledge of how to approach different tests. When you put it all together you create a strong potential for test-taking success.

It Takes Regular Practice

A basic premise of NO MORE TEST ANXIETY is that anxiety reduction, effective studying, and test-taking skills can only be fully mastered with regular practice. You cannot simply read about a method and know it fully. An intellectual understanding of what relaxation techniques are supposed to do won't help you know the difference between tense muscles and relaxed muscles.

Regular practice is vital. For the methods to be truly effective, your mind and body must experience the feelings, concepts and techniques in an intimate way. Establish a daily practice routine that won't interfere with the things you must do. Find a quiet place and time where you're not likely to be interrupted.

Plan to do one or more of the exercises every day. If this turns out to be too difficult a schedule to keep, create one that you can stick to more easily. Be sure you allow for periodic breaks. Your goal is to make it easy for yourself to learn new skills, not find yourself bogged down with one more thing to worry about.

The time required to learn and practice the various relaxation, study and test-taking techniques will vary depending upon the exercises, the effort you put into them, and your own ability to learn new skills. Give yourself whatever time you need.

Relaxation training is a two-part process. The first part is to not force the process. Allow it to unfold. You want to simply let go of the unwanted tension. The second part is developing easy and effective ways of doing the first part. You cannot "force" or "will" yourself to be relaxed and at ease. If this were possible, you would have done it long ago.

Getting the most from the different techniques presented in this book requires patience and persistence. It also calls for accepting and trusting your innate abilities, some of which you will discover as you progress through NO MORE TEST ANXIETY.

Achieving goals and experiencing success automatically increases your feelings of confidence and personal power. At the same time you'll be establishing the unconscious habit of "knowing" how it is to feel assured and at ease. You can confront and overcome challenges, and do it without the excess tension, worry or emotional upheaval that may have stymied or slowed your success in the past. You will feel more in control and better able to tolerate uncomfortable situations. Best of all, you'll be a successful test-taker.

ANXIETY AND YOU

Understanding Test Anxiety and Your Reactions To It

No one is born with a fear of taking tests. There is no gene for anxiety-about-tests, any more than there is a gene for fear-of-flying. You can overcome test anxiety. Almost two hundred years ago, the great German poet and philosopher Goethe wrote, "Whatever you can do, or dream you can, begin it." If one of your dreams is being able to take tests without sweaty palms, an upset stomach, and clogged thinking, then reading and following what this book has to say is a solid start toward achieving what you wish. Your strong desire for change will add momentum and inspiration.

Your first step is discovering what test anxiety is and how it affects you. Anyone who has experienced test anxiety knows that worry, stress and tension add to the difficulties of taking a test.

The physical and emotional reactions associated with anxiety can be very harsh. They often interfere with thinking and concentration.

John is a highly test-anxious engineering student. He described his mental state while taking tests as "trying to think through mud or concrete." He noted, "The more important a test is, the more difficult it is for me to think clearly." He spoke of studying for an upcoming exam "...while having every stray thought in the world zipping through my mind, one after another, with no way to stop them. It was like a whirlwind of thoughts and I couldn't control them."

Students who experience long term test anxiety speak of feeling "stressed out" at the mere thought of an upcoming exam. Some become physically ill, while others "space out." Still others find that no matter how many hours spent studying, once the exam begins nothing they read stayed in their minds. It felt like every fact and idea drained out of their minds, down their spines, and seeped out

the bottoms of their shoes onto the floor. Students express thoughts of, I am going to fail this exam." "I can't remember the answers. "I'm going to do badly, and prove how much of a failure I am, once again."

What is Your Test-Anxiety Level?

It's time for you to discover your personal level of test anxiety. The scale that follows will give you a measure of how anxious you become in test taking situations. The more you know about your thoughts, feelings and reactions to test anxiety, the better you'll be able to address and deal with them. You can complete the scale in less than five minutes.

For your own awareness and as a measure of your progress, take the scale now, before you begin to use the anxiety-reducing techniques described in each step. To gauge your rate of improvement, retake it two weeks into your program and again after one month. Remember: the difference between a little progress and marked improvement is a matter of practice and determination.

TEST ANXIETY SCALE

T	F		
			Answer True or False to the following questions.

❑ ❑   1. While taking an important exam, I find myself thinking of how much brighter the other students are than I am.

❑ ❑   2. If I were to take an intelligence test, I would worry a great deal before taking it.

❑ ❑   3. If I knew I was going to take an intelligence test, I would feel confident and relaxed.

❑ ❑   4. While taking an important examination, I perspire a great deal.

❑ ❑   5. During class examinations, I find myself thinking of things unrelated to the actual course material.

❑ ❑   6. I get to feeling very panicky when I have to take a surprise exam.

❑ ❑   7. During a test, I find myself thinking of the consequences of failing.

❑ ❑   8. After important tests, I am frequently so tense my stomach gets upset.

❑ ❑   9. I freeze up on things like intelligence tests and final exams.

❑ ❑   10. Getting good grades on one test doesn't seem to increase my confidence on the second.

❑ ❑   11. I sometimes feel my heart beating very fast during important exams.

❑ ❑   12. After taking a test, I always feel I could have done better than I actually did.

❑ ❑   13. I usually get depressed after taking a test.

❑ ❑   14. I have an uneasy, upset feeling before taking a final examination.

❑ ❑   15. When taking a test, my emotional feelings do not interfere with my performance.

❑ ❑   16. During a course examination, I frequently get so nervous that I forget facts I really know.

❑ ❑   17. I seem to defeat myself while working on important tests.

❑ ❑   18. The harder I work at taking a test or studying for one, the more confused I get.

❑ ❑   19. As soon as an exam is over, I try to stop worrying about it, but I just can't.

❑❑ 20. During exams, I sometimes wonder if I'll ever get through school.

❑❑ 21. I would rather write a paper than take an examination for my grade in a course.

❑❑ 22. I wish examinations did not bother me so much.

❑❑ 23. I think I could do much better on tests if I could take them alone and not feel pressured by time limits.

❑❑ 24. Thinking about the grade I may get in a course interferes with my studying and my performance on tests.

❑❑ 25. If examinations could be done away with, I think I would actually learn more.

❑❑ 26. On exams I take the attitude, "If I don't know it now, there's no point worrying about it."

❑❑ 27. I really don't see why some people get so upset about tests.

❑❑ 28. Thoughts of doing poorly interfere with my performance on tests

❑❑ 29. I don't study any harder for final exams than for the rest of my course work.

❑❑ 30. Even when I'm well prepared for a test, I feel very anxious about it.

❑❑ 31. I don't enjoy eating before an important test.

❑❑ 32. Before an important examination, I find my hands or arms trembling.

❑❑ 33. I seldom feel the need for "cramming" before an exam.

❑❑ 34. The university should recognize that some students are more nervous than others about tests and that this affects their performance.

❑❑ 35. It seems to me that examination periods should not be made such intense situations.

❑❑ 36. I start feeling very uneasy just before getting a test paper back.

❑❑ 37. I dread courses where the instructor has the habit of giving "pop" quizzes.

Scoring the Test Anxiety Scale is very easy. The total number of true answers is your test anxiety score. A score of 12 or below ranks in the low test anxiety range. If that is your score, the chances are you wouldn't be looking at this book now. A score of

Test Anxiety Scale reproduced from Sarason, I. G. (1980), Test Anxiety: Theory, Research and Applications. Permission granted by Lawrence Erlbaum Associates, Inc.

12 to 20 ranks in the medium range. Any score above 20 signifies high test anxiety. Scoring 15 or greater is a good indication you experience considerable discomfort about taking tests.

A high test anxiety score is not cause for alarm. Scoring in the medium to high range simply means that everything you learn from NO MORE TEST ANXIETY will be very useful. You can overcome excessive anxiety. The seven steps that follow present many different methods for lowering your test anxiety score.

You may find that some of the techniques and exercises in this book produce dramatic results. More often, changing the way you respond to pressure and stress will take time. Deep and lasting change rarely happens instantly.

ANXIETY IN GENERAL

Anxiety is generally defined as the mental, emotional and physical responses you experience when you anticipate that something bad or dangerous is about to happen. You believe you'll lose control, and that makes for very uncomfortable feelings.

What Test Anxiety Is and Is Not

Remember when you had to present a paper before your class, or when you were about to go on stage for the first time in the class play? Do you recall how scared you were, and the knot of fear that settled in your stomach? You were experiencing "stage fright," the same anxiety suffered by actors, athletes, and public speakers.

Test anxiety is form of performance anxiety. Anticipating that you'll do badly on an exam generates a fear of failure. The anticipation of failing brings feelings of worry, anxiety, and stress.

Actually, as long as it is not excessive, worry serves a useful purpose. It helps your mind focus on a current problem or difficulty so you can find an effective solution. Worrying is a problem only when it becomes a block to clear thinking. Then, worry strengthens and perpetuates your anxiety. After a while, constant worrying can turn into a pattern that tends to repeat itself endlessly.

5

Chronic Test Anxiety

Richard was a twin. His sister always got high grades without trying, and his parents couldn't understand why Richard's grades weren't as good. Janice has never gotten over a third grade teacher who harshly pointed out every word she mispronounced when she read in front of the class. As far back as he can remember, Stu could never get a grade good enough to please his father.

People with chronic test anxiety have generally had difficulties with test and performance fears for a long time. Studies indicate that chronic test anxiety frequently begins in early youth. The pattern can be initiated when a child is repeatedly exposed to criticism or other negative messages from important adults such as parents or teachers. The message the child takes in is, "Don't succeed." In time, the child may learn to anticipate failure. Failure is painful for anyone, and painful feelings often lead to anxiety.

When something makes you anxious your natural desire is to avoid it. To escape feeling anxious, any child becomes less and less inclined to attempt new or unfamiliar tasks. After failing enough times, you'll avoid any task that even suggests the possibility of failure. Like touching a hot stove, after you've been burned a few times you stay away from the stove. Get burned too many times, and you'll probably stay out of the kitchen as well.

Situational Test Anxiety

Jonathan graduated with honors from UCLA and Harvard Law School. Tests didn't bother him. However, he panicked when it came to preparing for the California bar. His concern was that this one test stood like a huge barrier between him and everything he had worked so hard to achieve.

Once he overcame his anxiety, he could get past that last big hurdle and enjoy a much deserved success as a practicing attorney.

In contrast to students with chronic test anxiety, students with situational test anxiety do quite well on most tests but encounter difficulties on "The Big One" such as the SAT, GMAT, a medical board, the bar, or a qualifying test for a new job. They worry that doing badly on a particular exam will cause damage to their education or career, and somehow jeopardize the rest of their lives. Worry causes that special test to assume awesome importance.

Situational test anxiety is specific to a particular event. High school students must achieve a score on the SAT that meets or exceeds a certain standard if they want to get into the college or university of their choice. College students need a sufficiently high score on the GRE, GMAT, LSAT or whatever to meet graduate school admission requirements.

Law graduates taking the bar, doctors facing medical boards or individuals encountering job placement exams are in the same situation. They think a poor score means their entire future is compromised. For these people, after spending years in preparation, blowing the exam means they can't practice or work as a professional.

THE MENTAL AND EMOTIONAL SIDES OF TEST ANXIETY

Regardless of whether you suffer from chronic or situational test anxiety, the end result is the anxious feelings that come with a very strong fear of failure. People experience test anxiety in different ways and with different degrees of emotional and physical distress. Recent studies strongly suggest that test anxiety is composed of two major components, emotionality and worry.

The Emotional Side

Your physical reactions express the emotional part of anxiety. These are the body responses that you commonly interpret as fear or distress. They include:

- Tight shoulder and neck muscles
- Tension headaches
- Butterflies in your stomach
- Tightness in the small of your back
- Sweaty palms
- Stress symptoms that are unique to you

The emotional ingredient has a rather diffuse and fleeting quality. It is sometimes difficult to accurately identify. One explanation is that your physical body doesn't know the difference between anxiety and excitement. The two states of arousal are exactly the same. It's your mind that decides whether a situation is exciting or anxiety provoking.

Your level of arousal depends on how important the coming test is to you. It is normal and helpful to feel aroused before a big test. Emotions get in the way only when you worry instead of being excited. Then you are likely to experience anxiety.

Students describe being increasingly upset and nervous as finals or other important exams approach, followed by a decrease in the level of their anxiety and a sense of relief after the exam is over. They continue to worry about the grade they might receive, but the students' level of emotional upset is much less than before they took the test.

The Worry Part

Of the two components of test anxiety, the most difficult to deal with is worry. It is the cognitive part of test anxiety, and includes thoughts and concerns about performance as well as fears about failure. Worry also represents the reasoning patterns an individual uses in every-day living. For these reasons, excessive worry is considered the root cause and chief sustainer of test anxiety.

In addition, continued worrying sets a vicious cycle into motion. The more the worry, the stronger your emotional arousal. The more aroused you become, the stronger your fear and worry. The unhappy end result: you find yourself progressively more anxious.

Worry and anxiety interfere with short-term memory, your ability to retain information for small periods of time. Short-term memory holds information only briefly while you need it. For example, you might repeat a phone number over and over until you write it down. Then you can release the number from your memory. A history date needed for an exam is another example; once the test is over, the date can vanish from your mind.

Test-anxious individuals have learned to believe that they will do poorly. Irrational worrying leads to a distorted self-image and an inaccurate perception of themselves. The result is often poor self-esteem. An important element in overcoming test anxiety is learning to identify and change harmful and negating self-concepts, You do this by introducing positive self-statements and images.

Students with low test anxiety are consistently able to focus more clearly on the test and its design, cues, and questions. When they don't immediately know answers, they are able to exercise sound deductive reasoning and good guessing strategies. They use efficient and effective study skills, minimize mistakes, and are able to maintain a high performance level. They build on the experience of success. They believe they will do well -- and they do. One success leads to the next and each success breeds greater confidence.

Mastering the techniques and exercises in NO MORE TEST ANXIETY helps change your self-image from one who cannot succeed to one who can. You'll break the cycle of worry and distorted thinking that is the underlying foundation of your test anxiety.

HOW ANXIETY AND STRESS ARE CONNECTED

If you are hiking in the woods and suddenly encounter a bear, every part of you will be instantly aroused to the danger staring you in the face. Your body will be prepared to fight or flee. You will be able to run faster or climb a tree quicker than you ever imagined.

Anxiety is experienced as a combination of mental and physical reactions. Your mind automatically interprets worry and anxious feelings as signs of danger. It triggers your body to react as it would in any dangerous or highly stressful situation. Facing a test becomes the same as facing an angry bear. You feel at risk.

Highly test-anxious students experience the same physical reactions to an upcoming exam as they do in any dangerous or risky situation. While a test is definitely stressful, it is not life threatening. However, your body doesn't know the difference.

It's a Natural Reaction

Stress is your body's natural response to any change. It is an every day fact of life and a part of living. You need some stress in order to function, to walk, move, and do every-day things. Stress can be purely physical, like moving from one place to another, or it can be entirely mental, like how you expect to do on a coming exam. In other words, stress can be positive as well as negative.

An example of a negative stress producer is looking in the rear-view mirror while driving and seeing a police car with its red lights flashing. Another is finding that someone has dented your new car, or when you expect to get a bad grade on an important test.

Positive life changes also produce stress. Winning the lottery, getting all A's, or riding a roller-coaster can create stress. Regardless of how it is perceived, stress is experienced as a combined physical and emotional response to something in your life, some change that is happening to you, in reality.

On the other hand, stress caused by anxiety is about something that has not yet happened. Anxious feelings arise when you think about or imagine something that may occur, and *you believe it will end badly*. It is when you "know" you won't achieve the SAT score needed to get into the college you've chosen, or when you "expect" that special person to reject you. You anticipate the worst, even though the results may be very different.

The mere anticipation of failure or rejection leads to heightened anxiety. This is anxiety generated from fantasy and imagination, and not based on a clear view of reality. Nonetheless, your physical reaction is as real as if danger was immediate and close at hand.

Your Body's Response to Stress

Picture a time when you were driving your car on a busy freeway or highway. Perhaps it was rush hour and the traffic was heavy. Suddenly the drivers in front of you had to stop and slammed on their brakes. You hit yours, and stopped just in time.

When those bright red brake lights abruptly flashed, how did you react? Did your hands tighten on the steering wheel as your foot quickly hit the brake pedal? Did your heart beat faster, your breathing become more rapid, and your mind become unexpectedly alert? Did you have time to think of fear while you were reacting?

The incident was over very quickly. The anticipated crash didn't happen. All of the stress reactions you experienced were a response to what you expected would happen. You may even have seen a picture of the crash in your mind as your foot mashed down on the brake pedal. Did you breathe a big sigh of relief? When did you know you were afraid? In all likelihood, not until it was over and you realized you were safe. You experienced the anxious reaction before you become mentally aware of the danger. Your body reacted to the stress long before it registered in your mind.

It's All In Your Head

10-30-00

For centuries people have recognized that anxiety is a reaction to anticipated risk. In the first century A.D. the noted Roman senator Lucius Annaeus Seneca said, "We are more often frightened than hurt; and we suffer more from imagination than from reality." For most people, anxiety is triggered by what they anticipate will happen rather than by what actually occurs.

One major difference between anxiety due to real risk and anticipatory anxiety is the way in which you release the anxious feelings. A dangerous situation has a clearly defined beginning and ending; the danger arises and eventually passes. You are relieved once you're safe. Anxiety caused by what you expect to happen has no clear end-point. After the test is over, your anxiety moves to the expected poor grade, feelings of failure, and the next exam.

CHANGING YOUR RESPONSES TO TEST ANXIETY

How do you relieve your worry, calm your emotions, and generate new ways of responding to anxiety and stress? Which approach works best? Where and how do you begin?

Clearly, overcoming test anxiety means that something has to change. Since the tests are going to remain fairly much the same, what must be altered is your approach to taking tests.

Reducing test anxiety and stress reactions to a comfortable level means learning to alter the way your body feels, from being tight and rigid to calm and relaxed. The ways in which you think about yourself and your abilities have to change from expectations of failure to the anticipation of success.

Efficient study skills are essential, just as knowing how to approach different types of tests to take advantage of the individual test design can be a real asset. Putting together all the various techniques and suggestions in NO MORE TEST ANXIETY can dramatically decrease your test anxiety, while significantly increasing your test scores.

The Circular You

Human beings respond to the world around them in basically three ways: they *think*, they *feel*, and they express their thinking and feeling with *actions*. When you are happy you feel good, your thoughts are light, and your actions are relaxed. Sadness brings gloomy thoughts, down feelings, and spiritless behavior. Stressful situations cause worried thinking, anxious feelings, and tense activity.

In order to respond differently to a particular situation, you need to make a change in one of the three response modes described above. It doesn't matter which way of responding you address first. Since all three modes are interconnected, each influences the others. An easy way to understand the concept is to look at the illustration shown below.

The circle represents you, and the black squares represent the three basic modes in which you can respond in any situation. The circle also illustrates the fact that thinking, feeling, and behaving are not separate functions operating independently of each other.

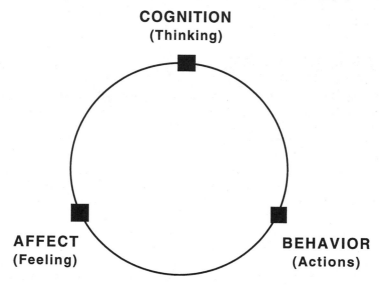

COGNITION
(Thinking)

AFFECT
(Feeling)

BEHAVIOR
(Actions)

For example, when you feel happy your thinking is positive and "up," and there is a bounce to your step. You do things in a positive frame of mind. Angry thoughts are usually accompanied by tense muscles and upset feelings. Your physical actions may be jerky and your speech quite abrupt. Sadness is usually accompanied by more quiet behavior and slowed thinking.

You want to reduce test-anxiety and regain control. The easiest way to break the anxiety-cycle is to use your body. Getting relaxed is not difficult for most people. Letting go of tension and relieving anxious feelings is one thing you are designed to do very well.

Just Let It Happen

The nice thing is that your body relaxes best when you don't work at it and just let it happen. Telling you to let something happen implies that you know what to do. The implication is correct.

It may come as a surprise, but you already possess an innate knowledge of how to achieve deep states of relaxation and inner peace. You were born instinctively knowing how; it's just that you may have forgotten some of the details.

The exercises in NO MORE TEST ANXIETY will help you remember how to use your forgotten skills and abilities. The techniques and exercises are designed to assist you in changing your mental, emotional, and physical reactions to testing and other stress-producing events.

Using What You Learn

Dick is a high school senior and a good athlete. He was playing in a baseball game that was held away from home. It was the bottom of the ninth inning. His team had two men on base and trailed the opposition by one run. The opposing team's fans put up a terrific uproar as Dick came to bat. The tension he felt was almost unbearable.

As Dick stood at the plate and focused intently on the pitcher, he spontaneously created a kind of mental bubble that included only the pitcher and himself. Everyone and everything else was left out. Within this narrow corridor of vision, his focus and concentration were suddenly more acute. He no longer felt the excess tension or heard the fans shouting. Nothing distracted him.

The story may sound like a movie, but Dick got the hit that scored the winning run. He reported that an awareness of the crowd and the noise did not return until he had safely reached first base. Dick used the same concentration technique in his sport that he learned for studying and taking tests.

ANXIETY AND LEARNING DISORDERS

Anxiety is common in students with test anxiety. It is also very evident in students with learning disorders. This is where the similarity ends. The presence of anxiety is not an automatic indicator of a learning disability.

Like actors, many students have anxiety before performing or taking a test. For them, the fear of doing badly is the direct cause of their anxious reactions. Anxiety is uncomfortable. Students with high test anxiety often want to avoid studying and tests altogether.

If your anxiety about taking tests is part of a continual, long-term anxious reaction to school and learning, the possibility that you have a learning disorder should be considered. A history of difficulties with focusing, concentrating, reading, writing, understanding or remembering indicates that you may have a problem with focusing or with processing information.

Many factors other than learning disorders can be involved when learning is problematic. If you feel your anxiety is about more than taking tests, you should contact a learning disorders specialist for an accurate diagnosis. You will find more information about identifying learning disorders in Appendix A.

LISTENING AND DOING

I encourage you to use the CD that comes with NO MORE TEST ANXIETY. It contains a number of the breathing, relaxation, studying and auto-hypnosis scripts you will find throughout the book.

There are clear advantages to using the CD. Some of the exercises and visualizations are rather long and involved. Listening to the CD relieves the pressure of trying to remember the wording or exact sequence of an exercise. All of your focus can be on the experience; there is much less chance of becoming distracted, missing a step or doing the various steps in an exercise out of order.

Go With The Voice

Students report that using the CD makes the exercises more effective and easier to learn. Without the CD or an audio tape, their concentration was disturbed each time they had to check the book to read what came next. In addition, listening to the CD helps you to "get into" the exercises more fully. Your experience will be very immediate, richer, and more complete.

❶ Allow yourself to go with the suggestions. Flow with the sensations. The experience should simply occur, so don't attempt to force anything to take place. To repeat, deep relaxation is a process of letting go and allowing something to happen.

❷ To help you study in a more relaxed mode, you'll hear the suggestion that when you open your eyes, your mind will be ready for action, while your body remains calm and at ease. You'll be surprised at how well that paradoxical thought works for you.

❸ Use ending suggestions that extend your relaxation period, or prepare you for studying in a calm and open frame-of-mind.

Recording Your Own

If you like the sound of your own voice or want the experience of making your own audio tapes using the scripts in the book, there are specific techniques to be aware of when you're recording.

❶ The exercises should be read in a slow, calm, and relaxed voice, with no dramatic rise or fall in tone or volume. Your goal is to achieve a state of peaceful calm, not heart-racing excitement. Do not rush your words.

❷ You can judge your vocal speed by reading in rhythm with your breathing. Inhale easily and naturally, and say the words into the recorder as you exhale. Pause at the end of each sequence where you see the three dots (...) to allow time for you, when you are the listener, to comply fully with the suggestions. As much as possible, put yourself into the experience.

❸ Allow yourself to feel what you are suggesting as you speak the words. When you listen to the tape, the emotional overtones will enhance and deepen the relaxation experience for you.

❹ How you finish the exercise or visualization depends on what you want to do next. You might wish to play the tape each night while in bed and just before going to sleep. In that event, simply tell yourself that when the tape stops you'll drift off into dreamland and awaken refreshed, relaxed and ready to perform.

❺ On the other hand, if you intend to hit the books after you have finished listening to your tape, a different ending technique is required. You must add some sense of activity to be sure your mind is fully alert and aware when you end the relaxation session. You can do this by raising your voice in volume and tone, and speaking more quickly as you tell yourself to "return to this time and place." You can also add a suggestion on the tape that your mind is becoming "more alert, aware and awake, with energy flowing through your mind and body."

❻ Speaking louder and more rapidly are ways of telling yourself it is time for the relaxation session to end. Another way to end a session is to count backwards in your mind from ten to one, telling yourself that at the count of one you will be fully alert and aware.

Ordering Additional Audio CDs or Tapes

You can send for additional CDs, or one or more of the various audiotapes listed in the order section in Appendix B. The tapes include a number of different relaxation, visualizing, studying and auto-hypnosis exercises found throughout the book, and some that are not in the book.

SUMMING UP

Now that you understand how test anxiety interferes with thinking and concentration, you are ready to do something constructive about changing it. The First Step: Breathing, will show you how easy it is to use what you do naturally. Correct breathing will enable you to achieve a surprisingly deep level of relaxation. You will also find that your mind is less cluttered and you are able to think more clearly.

Step 1: STARTING AT THE BEGINNING

Breathing Correctly (and naturally)

AIR:

It supports and sustains life, and is absolutely essential for clear thinking and relaxed test-taking.

Correct breathing is the foundation for physical relaxation, and a major part of feeling peaceful and in harmony with the world around you.

Everyone begins life with an instinctive knowledge of the right way to breathe. The goal of Step 1 is to help get you back in touch with the easy, natural breathing you did as an infant. Every part of you benefits when you breathe correctly. More oxygen gets supplied to your brain and other vital organs. The act of breathing takes less effort. Thinking is easier because you experience less anxiety. All this results from an on-going body activity that is automatic, largely unconscious, and usually taken for granted.

In any situation, breathing directly affects all the physical and mental reactions your body experiences. When you feel happy and excited, your breathing is open, full, and exhilarating. When you face a big test and feel threatened or at risk, certain abdominal muscles automatically become tense. These muscles transmit signals to your brain which quickly interprets them as a sign of danger. Any indication of risk generates anxious feelings.

Breathing Away the Signals

Research has found that if your abdominal muscles don't become tense, no signals get transmitted and you don't "know" anxiety in your mind. The techniques presented in this chapter teach you to breathe and relax more naturally. Correct breathing relaxes your stomach muscles and short-circuits the anxiety signals. No signals, no anxiety.

As you learned in the previous chapter, planning a vacation or an outing to Disneyland, or preparing to enter a lion's cage, your body generates the same responses. The difference is in the way your brain interprets what it expects to happen. For a pleasurable activity your brain thinks, "No danger and no reason to be alarmed. It's fine to be relaxed and have a good time." If it is test-taking-time, the message sent out is, "Storms ahead. Sound the alarms and man the battle stations."

Breathe Like a Baby

A deep breath initiates every human being into the world. Every breath that follows is automatic and natural. A healthy infant's relaxed breathing is instinctively deep, easy and rhythmical.

Everyone breathes, yet few do so in the effortless, deep pattern they did as a newborn or young child. Take a moment to remember the last time you saw a very young child asleep. Did you notice what part of the child's body moved as it breathed? If you answered, "The stomach," you were right. An infant breathes in the easiest, most natural and efficient way. As the child fills its lungs with air, only its stomach moves, not the chest and shoulders. The infant breathes with its diaphragm, the large band of muscle that separates the chest from the abdomen.

When you breathe naturally, your diaphragm moves in and out. This muscle movement allows your rib cage and lungs to expand and contract. The expanding rib cage is your body's natural signal to exhale. If you find that you breathe mostly with your chest and shoulders, try to think back to when your breathing was easier and more natural. You may not be able to remember such a time.

However, you can be sure that when you were very young, you breathed in a completely natural and virtually effortless way. In fact, you allowed your body to do the breathing for you. If you have a friend or relative with a very young child, notice how the child breathes when it is asleep or at rest. Compare how the infant breathes with the way you breathe now. Is there a difference? If so, what do you see?

Your Breathing Tells a Tale

Breathing is one of the few body functions that can be either voluntary or involuntary. You can consciously regulate your breathing, or you can ignore it and breathe with no awareness at all.

However, paying attention to your breathing can quickly tell you a lot about yourself. Your breathing pattern reflects whatever mental and physical events are taking place in your life at any given moment. If you feel down and dejected, your breathing will be shallow, rather jerky and will probably include deep sighs. Pain induces a sharp intake of breath, a gasp. Excitement and enjoyment cause your breathing to be quicker and less deep, but still relaxed. When you are calm, your breathing is smooth, rhythmical, and easy.

Natural Breathing

Conscious, natural breathing is necessary for controlling stress. It is also central for developing focus and concentration. Learning to again breathe naturally is the first step on the path to anxiety reduction and complete relaxation. Modifying test anxiety can begin with changing your pattern of breathing. All the exercises and techniques described in this book use diaphragmatic breathing as a core element.

Easy, natural breathing is very soothing and seems effortless. In contrast, it takes real effort to breathe when you are tense. Anxious breathing uses a lot more energy than breathing naturally because when you breathe your abdominal muscles are rigid.

With your stomach muscles constricted, you breathe in quick, shallow bursts of air using only the upper third or half of your lungs. The only muscles left for breathing are the ones in your chest and shoulders. The rest of your lungs remain either partly or completely empty of oxygen. You still take in all the oxygen you need, but you are breathing very inefficiently.

People who breathe only in their upper chest by using their chest and shoulder muscles will inhale and exhale an average of sixteen to twenty times per minute. Those that breathe using their diaphragm will average only six to eight breaths per minute. This may not seem important until you extend the numbers over a twenty-four-hour period. Chest breathers will average 22,000 to 25,000 breaths. In comparison, natural breathers will average 10,000 to 12,000 breaths. Now you have a significant difference.

Breathing with your diaphragm uses much less energy and effort. That means more energy is available for the mental tasks of thinking, learning, memorizing and remembering. Plus, focusing completely on your breathing for just a few moments reduces anxious feelings and encourage a sense of calm and well-being.

LEARNING TO BREATHE

How naturally do you breathe? More important, do you know how to breathe naturally? The following exercise tells you more about your breathing. It will help you remember how to breathe correctly. You'll learn to re-establish the effortless way you breathed when you were a young child.

As you do the exercise, be sure to breathe through your nose and not through your mouth Pay attention to two different sensations. First, focus on how your breathing feels. Notice the air as it flows through your nostrils, down your throat and into your lungs. Second, note the movement of your hands. How much do they move, and in what direction? You may find that your hands move individually or together, up and down, in and out, or a combination of all the ways. Closing your eyes will help eliminate distractions and allow you to focus more clearly on what you're about to experience.

❶ Sit in a comfortable chair with your back supported and both feet on the floor. Place one hand on your chest. Place the other hand on your abdomen, and let it rest on the large diaphragm muscle just above your waist.

❷ Take in a deep breath of air, filling your lungs as completely as you can. Feel your rib cage open as your lungs expand to their fullest capacity. Hold the breath for a brief moment and then exhale completely.

Did both hands move or only one? If only one moved, was it the hand on your chest or the one on your stomach? In what direction did it move, up and down, in toward your spine and out, or was it a combination of both movements?

❸ Take another deep breath. Briefly hold the air in your lungs. Now breathe out, and as you do so, again focus on the feelings and the movement of your hands. How do you feel? How much air were you able to take into your lungs? Exhale completely.

A Different Way of Breathing 1-17-6?

Now you'll experience breathing in a different way. Sit comfortably with both feet on the floor and with your hands placed on your chest and abdomen as you did before. While doing the following exercise, notice again how this way of breathing feels, and in which direction your hands move.

You know you have two lungs, but for this exercise imagine you have only one. In your mind's eye, visualize that one lung in the shape of a large cylinder. It is located in the middle of your torso, and extends from your neck to your waist. See the cylinder divided into three equal parts. You are going to fill the cylinder with air.

Focus on filling the cylinder as follows: first fill the bottom part, then the middle, and lastly the top. When you exhale you will empty the cylinder in the reverse order: top, middle, and then the bottom. Many people find that imagining they are breathing air in through their navel helps to fill the bottom of the cylinder first, since the navel is closest to the bottom of the cylinder-lung.

❶ Begin to take a deep breath of air through your nostrils. Relax your stomach muscles as you draw the air in to fill the lowest third of the cylinder. Feel the hand resting on your diaphragm moving forward and then inward as you continue to inhale.

❷ Now fill the middle third of your lungs and, as you do so, notice how your rib cage expands outward. As your stomach pulls in, feel your diaphragm moving slightly inward toward your back.

❸ Lastly, fill the upper third of the cylinder. Feel, and in your imagination, see the air filing your cylinder-lung completely. As your rib cage expands to its fullest your shoulders may rise slightly and move backward. Notice the hand on your chest moving up and out in unison with your chest muscles.

❹ Hold the breath for a few seconds and enjoy the healthy feeling of your chest open and fully expanded.

❺ Exhale completely and smoothly. Feel the warmed air as it passes through your nostrils. Expel the air from the upper part of the cylinder/lung first, progressing through the middle and then the bottom part. You may notice your shoulders dropping slightly and feel your rib cage contracting as you gently yet firmly forced the air out of your body.

❻ When you have expelled all the air you can, visualize a candle about a foot in front of you. Attempt to blow it out with any air that remains in your lungs. Now you have exhaled completely.

❼ Repeat the complete breathing-exhaling process one or two more times to become familiar with it. Then, stop taking deep breaths and let your breathing to return to its normal pattern.

How much more air could you take in by breathing this second way? Which way did your hands move? Most students report being able to inhale much more air when they used this cylinder-lung method than when breathing as they usually do with their chest and shoulders. Sit quietly and breathe normally. Notice how effortless your breathing can be when you allow your diaphragm to do the work for you, the way it was designed to.

Correct breathing uses your entire lungs rather than only the upper third of the lung area. Perhaps it surprised you to discover how much more air you could take in when you breathed deeply using your diaphragm. You may also have noticed how much less the hand on your chest moved up-and-down, while the hand on your diaphragm moved in-and-out.

It's Effortless

Diaphragmatic breathing is completely natural and feels very different from chest and shoulder breathing. It is much more relaxed. There is a forced quality to breathing done only in the chest, perhaps because chest breathing uses many more muscles and much more energy. When you breathe naturally and correctly, you use *only* your diaphragm muscle for inhaling and exhaling.

Smooth breathing enhances relaxation. In some of the breathing exercises that follow I will ask you to alter the flow and pressure of the air as you draw it into your lungs. You are relearning to breathe naturally, and as evenly and smoothly as possible.

■ As you breathe with your diaphragm, concentrate on making each breath smooth and steady. The flow and pressure of the air through your nostrils and throat should be even and continuous throughout the entire cycle.

■ Breathing with your diaphragm may seem strange at first, especially if you have been inhaling and exhaling with your upper chest and shoulders for a long time. Practice relaxed breathing regularly, at least two to three times each day. I recommend that each practice session last for approximately five to ten minutes.

■ Strive to make relaxed, diaphragmatic breathing your normal breathing pattern. Natural, rhythmic breathing is one of the most important and effective relaxation technique you can learn.

Use the Quiet Time

In all the breathing exercises, be aware of the quiet time at the end of each exhale. This is the calmest point in the breathing cycle. It is the brief period of time that occurs after you have finished exhaling one breath and before you begin to inhale the next breath. Feel the stillness in your body and quickly scan yourself from head to toe. Note any places of tightness or tension. As you inhale, imagine you are breathing into the tense area. With each exhale breathe the tight feeling out of your body. This is a way of using the quiet moment to reach an even deeper state of calm and comfort.

Your Inner Signal for Relaxation

Once you learn to use the full capacity of your lungs to inhale and exhale, you add a powerful step that helps get you to easy, natural relaxation and reduced anxiety. You're giving yourself an inner signal, a non-spoken cue to your mind and body to let go of excess tension. You're also setting up a responsive pattern between your mind and body that conditions you to begin relaxing more quickly. At the same time, you have given your mind a message to begin emptying itself of negative, irrelevant, or unwanted thoughts.

❶ Choose words or sounds for your inner signal that have meaning to you. Use a brief phrase such as *LET GO, BE CALM, GENTLY, RELAX NOW,* or any other words or sounds that feel right for you. Breathe deeply.

❷ As you begin to exhale and the air leaves your nostrils or mouth focus on the words or sounds. "Hear" them clearly in your mind. Give yourself the same message with each exhale.

❸ Besides signaling your mind and body to begin the process of relaxing, focusing on an inner signal moves your attention from whatever is happening outside of you, to what is going on inside of you. Now you can focus on an inner calmness, and not on stress producing images or thoughts.

❹ After three to four deep breaths return your breathing to an easy, effortless and natural rhythm. Breathe less deeply and stop repeating the inner signal. Focus on deepening your relaxation.

BREATHING WITH A PURPOSE

Most people breathe automatically, without giving this essential process a second thought. Breathing can be automatic, or it can be the gateway to a new experience of controlling tension and mastering new skills. Natural breathing can be relaxing all by itself. That is why all the relaxation, visualization, studying and test-taking exercises that follow begin with deep breathing and the sound of your personal inner signal.

There are many breathing techniques. Following are some that expand your ability to breathe naturally. Some are adaptations of Yoga breathing patterns. All have proven effective as aids to reduce tension and increase feelings of inner peace and calm. I urge you to experience them all. Identify those which work best for you. While you practice each breathing method, notice the coolness of the breath when you inhale in contrast to the warmth of the breath that you exhale.

The Cleansing Breath

This is a unique way of physically and emotionally eliminating tension and distractions from body and mind.

❶ Lie down or sit comfortably and allow your eyes to close. Take three or four deep breaths. Let your breathing return to an easy and natural rhythm.

❷ As you inhale, imagine that the air you are breathing is colored. It can be any color you choose. With each breath, visualize the colored air filling your body from the top of your head to the tips of your toes. Allow the colored air to occupy every cell in your body. See the air as very pure and cleansing. As it flows through you it picks up and moves any tension, distractions, or impurities.

❸ Now imagine an opening somewhere in your body. It can be any kind of opening you choose. It may be a natural opening or an imaginary one, a mechanical valve or the pores of your skin. When you see your body completely filled with the colored air, allow the valve or whatever you've imagined to open.

❹ As you exhale you can visualize the colored air slowly leaving your body through the imagined valve or opening. Just as the level of water in a bottle drops as you drink it, imagine the level of the colored air slowly dropping as it leaves your body. The level will drop from your head and progress downward to your toes.

❺ Visualize the level as it drops lower and lower. As the air flows out of the valve or opening with each exhale, it collects and takes with it any unwanted tensions, annoying aches and irritations, and removes them from your mind and body.

❻ Continue to breathe slowly and easily. See the colored air as it picks up and carries away excess tension and anything else you do not need at this time. Visualize the air flowing out of your body, cleansing it completely and leaving you feeling calmer, brighter, and lighter.

❼ After the air has completely left your body, sit quietly and enjoy the feelings of calm and tranquillity. When you are ready, allow your eyes to gently open. Reorient your thinking to the present.

How was this experience for you? What color(s) did you visualize? Does this color (or colors) have special significance for you?

The Clarifying Breath

This is a form of stimulating breathing that refreshes your entire body.

❶ Sit or stand in a relaxed posture but with a straight back.

❷ Inhale deeply, filling the lungs from bottom to top.

❸ Hold the breath for three to five seconds.

❹ Purse your lips to create a small hole and forcefully exhale a small puff of air.

❺ Hold for a count of two and exhale another puff. Continue to exhale in small, forceful puffs until you have emptied your lungs completely. Repeat for three to five complete cycles.

Notice how exhaling forcefully exercises the diaphragm and encourages deep breathing that fully expands the rib cage. Do this exercise by itself or in combination with other breathing exercises.

Energizing Breathing

A fun way to quickly becoming energized when you find yourself listless and dragging.

❶ Make yourself comfortable, close your eyes and take a few deep breaths. Allow your breathing to be easy and natural.

❷ See the sun in your mind's eye with its life-giving rays of white light that extend down to you. With each inhale imagine yourself breathing in the white sunlight. As it fills you, the light energizes and refreshes your entire mind and body.

❸ With each exhale feel the white light radiating through your body and mind. You may feel it pulsating and vibrant as you breathe in the light's power and vitality.

❹ Experiment with other images and colors to find the combination that gives you the strongest sense of energy, enthusiasm and well being. The colors may change each time you do the exercise depending on your mood or energy level. You may find that the colors and images have special meanings for you. Whatever color you see, simply accept it and allow the color to be.

4-4-8 Breathing

An ancient Yoga technique used for quickly achieving a state of calm and inner peace. Reputedly, this breathing pattern is an effective way to minimize or eliminate headaches. The exercise is very effective for reducing any anxious feelings. It helps promote calm by emptying your mind of distracting thoughts and images.

❶ Make yourself comfortable, either seated or lying down. Close your eyes and inhale very deeply. Hold the breath briefly and exhale completely.

❷ Inhale again, and as you do so, mentally count from one to four.

❸ Hold the breath. Count from one to four without exhaling.

❹ Begin to exhale, counting from one to eight. Time the exhalation so that when you reach the count of eight your lungs are completely empty of air.

❺ Without pausing, begin the next cycle by taking in another deep breath.

Repeat the sequence five times. If you run out of air while exhaling before reaching a count of eight, take a deeper breath and exhale more slowly. Concentrate only on the counting as you inhale and exhale. Be sure to fill your lungs fully and empty them completely when you exhale.

Breathing to Go to Sleep

You'll enjoy a way of breathing that helps you fall asleep more quickly and awaken feeling more rested.

Lie in bed comfortably, close your eyes and focus on the rhythm of your breathing. For this exercise, concentrate on exhaling approximately twice as long as you inhale. Use whatever breathing pattern works best for you. It may be that three breaths as you inhale and six as you exhale feel most comfortable, or four to inhale and eight to exhale, or whatever. The exact breathing pattern is not as important as the rhythm you establish. Also, you are not trying to completely fill or empty your lungs for this exercise.

Your breathing should be effortless and smooth. Eliminate any shakiness, pauses or stops as you inhale and exhale. Concentrate on a smooth and even flow of air in and out of your nostrils, and then breathe to the following counts.

❶ Count eight breaths lying on your back.

❷ Turn onto your right side and count sixteen breaths.

❸ Turn onto your left side and count thirty-two breaths.

Should you normally sleep on your right side, simply reverse steps ❷ and ❸ by first counting sixteen breaths on the left side and then thirty-two on the right side. If you concentrate totally on your breathing rhythm and the counting, you may find that you consistently fall asleep before finishing the exercise. So much the better.

Breathing Through Alternate Nostrils

Another ancient Yoga technique has been found to expand lung capacity, increase breathing control, and enhance concentration. Regardless of how long a breath you take, focus on breathing smoothly and evenly as you inhale and exhale.

❶ Sit comfortably in a chair or on the floor with your back straight but not rigid.

❷ Using your right hand, rest the index and middle fingers on your forehead and between your eyebrows. If you are left handed, simply use the fingers of that hand.

❸ Notice which nostril is most open. If it is the left , gently press your thumb against the right nostril to close it completely. If the right nostril is most open, use your ring finger to close the left nostril.

④ Breathe naturally through the open nostril for approximately thirty seconds.

⑤ Close that nostril as you open the other, and again breathe easily.

⑥ Alternate nostrils, breathing through the open one as you close the other.

⑦ Lower your hand and slowly resume natural breathing. A complete cycle is breathing through each nostril in turn.

⑧ Begin by doing five to seven cycles. As you become comfortable with the process, gradually increase to fifteen or twenty cycles.

Yoga practitioners believe that breathing through alternate nostrils increases lung capacity. It also improves concentration because you must focus intently as you do the exercise.

SUMMING UP

Natural and effortless breathing is an essential first step in achieving your goal of worry-free test-taking. Step One demonstrates that natural breathing minimizes the anxious feelings that often result from worry and stress.

Now that you have mastered the art of natural breathing, it's time to learn to reduce muscle tension. Step Two: Letting Go Of What You Don't Need, offers a number of different methods for achieving physical relaxation.

Step 2: LETTING GO OF WHAT YOU DON'T NEED

Relaxation
in mind and body

A lessening of or rest from work, worry, or effort;
A reduction of muscular tension

Webster's
New World Dictionary

Step One introduced correct breathing as the quickest way to start becoming relaxed. Step Two expands your efforts and brings you closer to your goal. You'll learn to relax the muscles that tense up when you are under stress. Relaxation counters the tension that lies at the core of anxiety. At the same time, it puts you back in control of what's going on in your body.

BECOMING AWARE

Most people don't know their bodies very well. They may be aware of many things, the day of the week, the home team's winning score, or where they are supposed to be at a certain hour. Yet, they aren't very observant about what happens within their own body.

Any approach to relaxation requires body awareness. Some individuals have become so used to tension, they they are no longer able to discriminate between muscles that are tense and those that are relaxed. They may consider tight muscles to be a "normal" state and find it strange to release the tension. They are used to living with tension, and at first, may experience relaxation as unusual and perhaps even uncomfortable.

Ted is a student at a large eastern university. He told me he couldn't remember a time when he wasn't primed and ready to "spring into action." Being tense was Ted's usual state, and he wasn't sure he wanted to know how to relax. His concern was that he would lose his "edge," a kind of alertness that he felt gave him an advantage in competitive situations.

Unfortunately, the "edge" or "alertness" Ted experienced was costing him much more than he realized. Staying constantly keyed up used so much tension and energy that he easily became fatigued. He had difficulty thinking clearly when he needed to, or even being able to relax enough to fall into a good sleep at night.

Tension Versus Relaxation

How well do you know your body and its responses? Are you aware of how and where you carry tension? Have you been tense for so long that you don't know what it feels like to be relaxed? Do you know when you are tense? Can you easily release muscle tension? Would you like to change your "normal" state from being tense to feeling relaxed?

Physical relaxation is basically a two-part process. The first part is recognizing when your muscles are tense. The second part is achieving muscle relaxation when you want to.

Conscious and voluntary muscle relaxation is based on a simple fact with a long name: reciprocal inhibition. The simple fact is that no muscle in your body can be tense and relaxed at the same time. It can be either in tension or at rest.

The idea is even more obvious and straightforward than it sounds. To illustrate: you know it's impossible to be in Los Angeles and New York at the same time. It is equally impossible for your muscles to be relaxed and tense at the same time. Prove the concept to yourself with the following, quick demonstration.

❶ Sit in a comfortable chair and allow your hands to rest on your thighs. With your dominant hand make a fist that is firm and tight, but not painful. Feel the tension in your hand and fingers, the wrist, and up into the forearm, elbow and upper arm.

❷ Without changing a thing, relax your hand. If you did not change anything your hand will still be clinched in a fist. Notice that as long as you maintain the same degree of muscle tension, you cannot relax your hand.

❸ Now, open your fist and relax the entire hand. Allow all tension to drain from the fingers, hand, wrist, and the lower and upper arm. Let your hand rest limply and comfortably on your thigh and notice the warmth as blood flows unrestricted through the fingers and hand.

❹ Then, without changing a thing, make a fist. If your hand remains truly relaxed and no muscles are tightened, you cannot introduce the tension that moves your fingers and hand into a fist.

You have just experienced reciprocal inhibition in action. Reciprocal inhibition is noteworthy because almost all emotional experiences require some corresponding physical involvement.

As you learned in Chapter One, if you don't experience tension in certain muscles, you can't experience anxiety. Since anxiety requires tight stomach muscles, relaxing those muscles reduces your anxious feelings. By reducing the anxiety you experience less worried thinking. When you worry less, you can relax more. Being relaxed increases your serenity. Peace of mind leads to clear thinking. This is the exact opposite of your anxiety cycle.

How do you experience anxiety? Do you feel it as tight muscles in your abdomen. Does the tension extend to your upper back and neck? Is it the sensation of fluttering butterflies in your stomach? Do you perceive it as a band of pressure around your chest? However you experience tension and stress, it involves tightened muscles. Tense muscles are your body's way of clearly stating you are experiencing stress.

Are you aware of muscle tension when you're worried? Can you identify the anxiety messages your body sends out? Progressive relaxation is designed to help you recognize the signals, and what you can do about the messages.

Progressive Relaxation

More than fifty years ago, Dr. Edmond Jacobson wrote, "An anxious mind cannot exist within a relaxed body...a state of reciprocal influence exists between the brain and body." His research showed that mental and muscle activities are interrelated, and that when muscles become relaxed brain activity and overall anxiety are reduced. By instructing people in tensing and then relaxing all the muscle groups in their bodies, he helped them overcome many stress-related illnesses.

Progressive relaxation has three aims. Each is distinctive and important. Their combined purpose is to help you recognize tension and its effects, and show you how to best reduce your anxiety.

Aim One: First and most important is for you to learn to distinguish between tension and relaxation. As you progress through each tension-relaxation phase, note the difference between muscles under tension and those that are relaxed.

Aim Two: The second goal is to note which other muscles become tense as you progress through the various muscle groups. Tense only the muscles on which you are focusing. Keep all other muscles as relaxed and tension-free as possible. Each time you do the exercises you'll find it easier to tense only the specific muscles you wish to, and achieve more relaxation when you let go.

Aim Three: The third goal is for you to be aware of how good it feels when you release the tension. You'll experience how comfort can grow and expand within your body as you progress through each of the relaxation phases.

Jacobson's original program of progressive relaxation took almost six months for an individual to complete. The version that follows is considerably condensed, yet still effective. You will be tensing and then relaxing each of sixteen muscle groups throughout your body. Do the groups in the order in which they are presented.

Tense each set of muscles for about seven seconds. After holding the tension, completely relax the muscles for thirty to forty-five seconds. Do each step in the exercise twice before moving on to the next muscle group. The entire sequence should take fifteen to twenty minutes.

Complete each tension phase with the mental cue to relax or let go. Let your muscles relax all at once rather than gradually. This releases the tension more quickly and completely. Please note: Do not tighten any muscles to the point of pain. If any muscles are already strained or in any way injured, avoid all exercises that involve the injured area. Check with your doctor if you have any questions.

Experiencing Progressive Relaxation

Make yourself comfortable, either in a seated position or lying down. Allow your eyes to close and take a few deep breaths. Repeat your inner cue to relax as you exhale. Remember to breathe as you do the exercises. Do not hold your breath unless instructed to do so.

❶ Make a fist with your right hand to put the muscles of your hand and forearm into tension. As you tighten your fingers, concentrate on the sensations of tension that radiate through the hand, wrist and forearm. Hold, then relax the muscles completely. Take a deep breath. As you exhale release any remaining tension in the hand. Breathe easily and notice the warmth as blood again flows freely through the fingers. Repeat the exercise.

❷ Tense the biceps in your upper right arm by bending your arm at the elbow and flexing, much as a young boy does when he "shows off" his muscles. Hold for seven seconds, then relax the upper arm completely. Feel the relaxation and warmth as the blood flows through the muscles. Allow tension to drain from your body. Carefully notice the differences as you focus on the sensations of tension and letting go. Breathe deeply before repeating the exercise or going on to the next.

❸ Clench your left hand into a fist to tighten the muscles of the hand and forearm as you did with your right hand. Hold, and relax completely. Compare the right hand with the left. Is one more relaxed than the other? Did your right hand tighten as you made a fist with your left hand? Focus on keeping the right hand relaxed as you again tighten the left. Hold, and then release any tension as you relax the fingers and forearm muscles.

❹ Tense the biceps in your upper left arm by bending the arm at the elbow and flexing it the same way as you did with your right arm. Hold, and relax the muscles completely. Feel the deep relaxation in both hands and arms from the shoulders to the tips of your fingers. Notice the warmth as circulation flows easily, unrestricted by muscle tightness.

❺ To tense the muscles in the forehead and scalp, raise your eyebrows as high as you can. Push them firmly toward your scalp. Hold, then relax completely. With the release of tension, let the skin become smooth and calm. Repeat the exercise and be aware of the changes in skin sensations when you tighten your scalp and then "let go."

❻ Close your eyes tightly and wrinkle your nose firmly to tense the muscles in the middle of your face. Hold, then relax the muscles. Let all the tension flow from your nose, cheeks and eyes. Feel your eyes relaxing deep within their sockets. Were you able to isolate tension to the middle of your face and not extend it to your forehead or jaw? Which muscles become involved?

❼ By pressing your lips and teeth together and pressing your tongue against the roof of your mouth, you will tense the muscles in the entire lower face. Hold, and relax the muscles completely.

Did you feel the ache that seemed to begin at the back of your tongue and spread through the back of your mouth? Repeat the exercise, and notice your lips part slightly when you fully relax the lower facial muscles .

❽ You can tense all the muscles in your neck by attempting to move your head in all four directions at one time. Hold and relax.

Did your shoulder and upper back become involved as you tensed all the neck muscles? Repeat and experience the vibration in your jaw and neck. Relax. Could you feel the relaxation extend from your jaw down through your shoulders?

Take a break. Inhale five deep breaths, holding each for about five seconds. As you exhale, breath-out the words *CALM* or *LET GO* and then scan your body for any places that may be holding tension. Breathe the tightness out with each exhale and notice the feelings of really letting go. When you are ready, continue the exercise.

❾ To tense the large muscle groups in your upper back, pull your shoulders back firmly, as though you were going to touch them together behind you. Concentrate on the tension in your upper back, shoulders, and down the spinal column to your waist.

Keep your head and neck as tension-free as possible. Hold, then relax the muscles completely. Do it again, being careful not to strain too much. As you relax and exhale, allow your shoulders to let go of any tension. Enjoy the sensation of warm relaxation spread down your back and spine.

❿ By pulling your shoulders in front of you and tightening your stomach muscles, you will put all the muscles in your chest and abdomen into tension. You can't breathe when doing this exercise.

Focus on the tension that extends from your neck to your waist. As you hold the tension, pull the muscles in even a little more. Relax and breathe. Release any extra tension with each exhale. Arch your back slightly before repeating and moving on to the next exercise.

⓫ Raise your right leg slightly off the floor and tighten your thigh muscle. This will tense the muscles in your upper leg. Feel the tightness from your buttocks to your ankle. Hold, then drop your leg and relax completely. You may notice warmth in your thigh that flows down into the lower leg. This exercise will improve circulation in the upper leg muscles. Repeat, tightening the leg muscles even more. Breathe the tension out as you drop the leg and truly let go. Continue to breathe as the tension falls away.

12 Carefully tense your right calf by pointing your foot forward and curling your toes. Because of the strong chance of foot cramps hold the tension for only three seconds. Pay attention to the sensations in your toes, foot, ankle and calf. Relax the muscles completely and note any difference between your right and left legs. Tense the muscles again and then relax. Remember to breathe easily and naturally.

13 Point the toes of your right foot back toward your face. This will tense all the muscles in your right ankle and shin. Feel the tightness in the ankle and the top of your leg. Notice how the tension extends up into your thigh. Hold and relax completely, feeling the difference between the tension and relaxation phases.

14 Tense your left thigh as you did the right one. Hold, then drop the leg and let the tension drain away. Were you able to relax the left leg more completely than the right? Repeat the exercise. Take a deep and full breath. As you exhale, breathe out any remaining tension.

15 Carefully tense your left calf for three seconds as you did the right calf. Hold briefly to prevent the muscles in your foot from cramping. Relax and repeat the exercise. Each time you let go, feel more of the tension drop away.

16 Tense your left ankle and shin the same way as you did the right and then relax completely. Repeat this last Progressive Relaxation exercise. Focus on the feelings of relaxation in both feet. Sit comfortably and quietly for a few moments. Enjoy the relaxation flowing through your body. Breathe deeply and evenly.

You can repeat any part of the exercises as often as you wish. Notice the muscles you use for carrying tension. If it's a particular bunch such as the neck, shoulders, upper back or lower back, repeat the exercises for those muscle groups. It is helpful to be aware of this since they are probably the muscles you generally tense up when you're feeling anxious or under pressure. Those are the muscles that can act as your early warning signals. When they become tense you are getting your first indication that it is time to pay attention. They're telling you to relax, and do it at once!

LET GO COMPLETELY!

Now that you have learned the difference between tension and relaxation, it's time to have an all-at-once experience. You're going to tighten your entire body and then suddenly release the pressure. Enjoy the luxurious feeling as tension is instantly discharged.

❶ Take a deep breath and exhale. Inhale again, and fill your lungs as full as you can.

❷ Hold the breath, and tighten all your muscles simultaneously. Feel the tension throughout your body.

❸ Maintain the tension for a count of ten, then relax everything quickly and completely. Release all muscle tightness, everywhere.

❹ Breathe deeply and evenly. Notice the warmth that courses through your body as you let go, and how very good it feels when you release the tension from every muscle, all at the same time.

Were you able to let go completely? As you progressed through the exercises, did you notice any muscles that remained tense in spite of your best efforts? Was it easier to relax some parts of your body than others? Practicing the sequence of progressive relaxation exercises will help you become more sensitive to localized muscle tension. With increased sensitivity, you can break the anxiety chain before it becomes overwhelming and out of control.

Jacobson's program of progressive relaxation is a very active process. Purposely tensing and relaxing muscles throughout your body requires you to be conscious of exactly what is happening at every moment of the exercise. Another, less physically active, method of progressive relaxation utilizes your imagination in concert with your muscles. The method is known as Autogenics, and it is the next step in your program.

AUTOGENICS

In 1926, Dr. Johannes Schultz of Berlin published a paper describing a method for inducing relaxation that he called "autogenic training." His system evolved from hypnosis studies done with a variety of individuals. He found that certain words and phrases suggested relaxation to the unconscious mind, which then effectively expressed the relaxing thoughts in the muscles.

Simply stated, autogenics is a process of passive focusing and concentration, a way of letting whatever happens, happen. You need only maintain a relaxed sense of personal peace-of-mind and have no expectations about the physical, mental or emotional responses you may experience when doing the exercises.

Dr. Schultz wrote, "It is important that throughout this procedure you adopt a relaxed, passive, and casual attitude. You cannot force relaxation to occur. Just give up conscious control over your body and allow your bodily processes to flow naturally."

Using your natural ability to visualize, you are going to create a peaceful environment and comfortable physical sensations. As you focus and concentrate completely on the images, they will translate into true reality in your body. No physical effort is involved. The goal is passive concentration.

Letting Go and Giving In

The secret is in letting go and giving in to relaxation. Trying to make relaxation happen can only fail. Autogenics (or any relaxation, for that matter) is most effective when you allow yourself to respond without thinking or effort. Responses are quite immediate, and you'll know very quickly how effectively autogenics is working.

You're going to give yourself suggestions for experiencing two sensations, heaviness and warmth. The sensation of warmth relates directly to increased blood flow throughout your body, particularly in your extremities. During stressful periods blood flow in your hands and feet is constricted. Warmth via increased circulation is a relaxation response that counters these stressful reactions. Heaviness relates to the physical sensations that your muscles are relaxing and letting go.

Imagine and Feel

An essential part of the process involves imagining and feeling yourself in a safe, comfortable, and peaceful place. You can allow your imagination to take you anywhere you choose: the beach, the mountains, or a beautiful meadow on a warm spring day. It can be a location you have visited before or a fantasy place you create in your mind. Whatever or where-ever the peaceful scene you visualize, it will be the right image for you when you do the exercise. Should the scene shift or be different at your next autogenics practice session, simply go with it.

Don't worry about how you visualize. Some people are able to visualize scenes or actions in sharp detail and brilliant technicolor. Others cannot. It isn't necessary for you to see the images clearly or in vivid color. Having a "sense" of the image will do just fine. As you do the exercises, focus on the inviting and peaceful image you bring to mind. Fully experience any sensations of warmth, heaviness, and relaxation that arise in your muscles.

Do all the autogenic exercises at least twice a day. Experience the sensations for approximately thirty seconds and repeat each suggestion four times before moving on to the next. Pause between each phrase. Above all, don't rush. Enjoy the sensations. The more you "get into" the experience the more they'll do for you.

Experiencing Autogenics

Each session takes approximately ten to fifteen minutes. Find a quiet location where you will not be disturbed. Sit in a comfortable chair that supports your neck and head, or lie on the bed or floor with your legs slightly separated and your arms at your sides.

Close your eyes. Clear your mind and quiet your thoughts. If any intrusive thoughts persist, you might visualize them as leaves in a small stream, drifting lazily along and soon passing out of sight and out of your mind. Imagine your special place, and when it is clearly in your mind's eye, say to yourself:

❶ "I am at peace. My right arm is heavy and warm. My left arm is heavy and warm. My heartbeat is calm and regular. My arms are heavy. My arms are warm. My breathing is regular. My arms are heavy and warm. I am at peace."

Feel the heaviness in your arms. Notice the warmth. Everyone experiences autogenics differently. Some feel the heaviness more, others the warmth. However you experience it is the right way.

❷ "My neck and shoulders are heavy and warm. My neck and shoulders are heavy and warm. My breathing is calm. My heartbeat is regular. I am at peace. My neck and shoulders are heavy and warm. My neck and shoulders are heavy and warm. I am at peace."

Concentrate on the feelings of warmth. Focus on the warmth in your arms, neck and shoulders. Let any thoughts flow through you. Remember to breathe naturally and easily. Take a deep breath and exhale completely.

❸ "I am at peace. My chest is heavy and warm. My chest is

heavy and warm. My breathing is calm. I feel at peace. My arms are heavy and warm. My heartbeat is calm and regular. My chest is heavy and warm. I feel peaceful."

Notice the heaviness spreading downward. Be aware of warmth through your upper body, bringing a sense of ease and contentment. Feel the sense of peace spreading with the heaviness and warmth.

❹ "My legs are heavy and warm. My breathing is calm. I am at peace. My legs are heavy and warm. My legs are heavy and warm. My heartbeat is calm and regular. My legs are heavy and warm. My breathing is calm and regular. I am at peace."

Feel the heaviness in your thighs and legs. Remember to breathe slowly, deeply and evenly. Be aware of any sensations of temperature changes in your arms and upper body.

❺ "My abdomen is warm and calm. My heartbeat is calm and regular. I feel at peace. My abdomen is warm and calm. My abdomen is warm and calm. My breathing is calm. My abdomen is warm and calm. I am at peace."

Concentrate on warmth in your stomach. Allow the sensations of warmth to spread downward from your neck, shoulders and chest.

❻ "I am at calm and at peace. My forehead is cool. My heartbeat and breathing are calm and regular. My forehead is cool. I am at peace. My forehead is cool. My abdomen is heavy and warm. I feel at peace. My forehead is cool. I am at peace."

Give yourself two to three minutes of silent, peaceful relaxation before telling yourself to again be fully alert. Slowly open your eyes. Take a full, deep breath and gently stretch. How do you feel? How clear was your visualization? Did you experience warmth and heaviness? Did you find it difficult to let your thoughts go? How much more relaxed do you feel than when you began?

Autogenics is easy to learn. Practice produces successful results in a very short time. The advantage of autogenics is that you can use the technique almost anytime you have a brief break in your schedule. You can do it at your desk, between classes, in front of the television during commercial breaks, or whenever you start to feel tense.

Passive-Progressive Relaxation

Combine Autogenics and Progressive Relaxation and you get Passive-Progressive Relaxation. You'll induce deep relaxation by bringing together natural breathing, a focus on awareness, and an image of your peaceful, personal place. Passive-Progressive Relaxation allows you to slowly and easily reduce tensions as you progress from one part of your body to another.

Concentrate on releasing all tension as you maintain a state of

passive attention to your body and the images in your mind. You'll use what you've learned about deep and natural breathing, by using your breath to focus the visualization and exhale away tension and stress. As in autogenics, do not actively tense any muscles. Remain peaceful, relaxed, and unstressed throughout the exercise.

❶ Begin by sitting or lying in a comfortable position much as you did for the Autogenic exercises. Take a few deep, natural breaths, giving yourself your personal signal and telling yourself to let go of any excess tension as you exhale. You might imagine the tension in your muscles being blown gently out and away from your body. Allow the image of a special, peaceful place to come to your mind. See yourself relaxed and at ease in this restful inner place.

❷ Focus attention on your feet and lower legs and become aware of how the muscles feel. Take a deep breath and as you exhale, release any tension in your feet and lower legs. Let it "flow" away. Be aware of the differences between tension and relaxation. Focus on any sensations of heaviness and warmth in your feet and legs. Allow those feelings to begin spreading up your legs and through your body.

❸ Turn your attention to your knees and upper legs and again take in a deep breath. Exhale completely, breathing any stress or tension out of the muscles and away from you. Concentrate on any remaining tension you may encounter; inhale deeply and release the tense feelings as you exhale.

❹ Progress to your hips and buttocks, breathing tension out of the muscles and becoming aware of feelings of heaviness, warmth and relaxation. Even if you are not aware of it yet, the feelings began with your feet and are automatically flowing up your body. Notice how heavy and relaxed your feet, legs, hips and buttocks have become. Focus on any remaining tension you notice in these muscles. Send the tightness out and away from your body with the next warm breath.

❺ Shift your attention to your lower back. Release any undesired tension each time you exhale. Gently expand your focus to include your entire back and shoulders. With each breath, let go of any tightness or stress you may have stored in the muscles. Send the tension out and away from you. Visualize your special place with you in it. With each passing moment, see yourself becoming more and more deeply relaxed and at ease.

❻ Focus now on your stomach and chest. Take in a deep breath, allowing the air to fill your entire torso. Be aware of how your diaphragm moves in and out as your chest expands outward. Exhale completely and release every little bit of tension. Enjoy the pleasurable feelings of calm and well-being.

❼ Consider your arms and hands. Inhale fully and completely. As you exhale, release any tension from your arms and hands. Feel your arms become heavy and warm, too heavy to move and very comfortable. Focus on any residual tension. Breathe into the tension and, in your mind's eye, see your breath carrying it away as you exhale.

❽ Move your focus to your neck and head. Many people carry tension in their upper shoulders and in the back of their neck. Notice any feelings of tension that you have stored in your neck and up across the back of your head. Inhale fully and as you exhale, breathe the tension out of the muscles and out of you.

Feel your head sink into the supporting surface beneath it. At the quiet time of the next breath, the moments when you have completely exhaled and before you take in the next breath of air, note any tension that my remain. With the next exhalation, gently blow the tension away.

❾ Slowly moving down your face, notice your forehead, eyes, mouth and jaw. Tension is often stored in the muscles around the eyes and mouth. Focus on any tightness you find. Allow yourself to gently breathe away the tension with the next few breaths. Notice how very comfortable it feels as these muscles become fully relaxed and at ease.

⑩ Take a very deep and enjoyable breath. Feel the heaviness and warmth that has spread throughout your body. Experience the sense of complete relaxation you have achieved. Imagine your special place and see yourself fully at ease. Scan your body from head to toe, and if you find any pockets of tension, breathe them out now. Be aware of how comfortable and peaceful you feel.

Create a mental picture of yourself as you feel at this moment. Enjoy the feelings. When you are ready to resume your activities, take a deep breath, stretch fully, and open your eyes. Remember this image. Know that you can easily bring it to mind whenever you feel excess tension or anxiety beginning to build.

Recognize your new skills, and know that you can re-experience these feelings of comfortable relaxation any time you wish. Each time you practice this or any of the relaxation exercises, you'll release tension faster and more easily. Choose the exercises you like, *and do them...a lot!*

SUMMING UP

Visualizing is an important ingredient in relaxation. You used it as part of the exercises in this chapter to release tension and invite relaxation. Step Three: Seeing With Your Mind's Eye, focuses on expanding your natural abilities to visualize and create images. Use your imaging skills not only for relaxation, but also to expand your memory and enhance your ability to recall what you need.

Step 3: SEEING WITH YOUR MIND'S EYE

Tools for Visualizing

Making the simple complicated is commonplace, making the complicated simple, awesomely simple, that's creativity.

Charles Mingus

Susan is a second-year undergraduate student. She has test anxiety coupled with a vivid imagination. Susan says that before a test she has a "vision" of herself being nervous. She "sees" her efforts as fruitless and unsuccessful. She "pictures" other students knowing the answers she doesn't, and has "an image" of always disappointing her parents. Susan is locked into an image of failing.

Before and during a test, Susan's responses parallel the pictures in her mind. She experiences high levels of anxiety when studying, has difficulty thinking and remembering during tests, and ends up receiving a poor grade. What Susan envisions becomes actual.

VISUALIZATION AND REALITY

Your imagination can be a powerful asset or an equally powerful liability. An ability to visualize can help you improve your grades and be a source of comfort and self-confidence. At the opposite extreme, the images you create can focus around anticipated failure. Then, the images will induce fear and anxiety.

Much research and many studies confirm that the images you see in your mind are expressed through your body. One study found that images strongly influence what you experience mentally and emotionally, as well as physically. This response to images is known as the Perky effect, and perhaps you'd like to demonstrate it for yourself.

When you do this exercise, be sure the arm and hand holding the thread do not move. Also, when you visualize the button moving in a certain direction, really *see* it happening. Make your images as clear as possible.

❶   Attach a length of thread to a large button and hold the end of the thread with your thumb and forefinger.

❷   Visualize the button moving in a certain direction, say, back and forth across your body. (The button won't go up and down, but it will move side to side, front to back, and in a circle.)

❸   Focus on your image of the button moving. "See" the movement of the button using all your concentration.

❹   Bring the button to a stop, again using only visualization.

❺   Now, visualize the button moving in a circle. Experiment with other directions, and then make the button come to a stop.

"So," you may ask, "what does moving a button have to do with test anxiety." The answer is that the button and thread (actually a pendulum) demonstrate that what you see in your mind is actively reflected in your body.

Visualization and Test Anxiety

Professional athletes know this idea of using mental imagery very well. They are aware that performing at peak ability is every bit as much mental as it is physical. To illustrate, an Olympic-class shot-putter's performance was dramatically improved after he viewed films of himself in action. What he didn't know was that the film was altered by his coaches so that the metal ball his body and arm heaved into the air went an additional five meters more than the distance it was actually thrown.

He watched the film each night before going to sleep, and, without realizing it, saw himself putting the shot farther than he had ever done. You've probably already guessed the outcome. He won a gold medal in the 1968 Olympic Games with a performance that was five meters longer than his previous best effort.

You used imaging in some of the relaxation exercises in Steps One and Two. Step Three shows you how effective a tool visualization is for overcoming test related anxieties.

Test-anxiety is exacerbated when you expect to fail a test and visualize the failure-scenario in all its gory details. You react not to what is happening in reality, but rather to your expectation of what *you think* will happen.

In the true story of the Olympic shot-putter, the athlete believed the images of the shot traveling an extra five meters. In the same way, your image of what will occur on a test can dramatically influence both your performance and the test results you achieve.

SEEING THE PICTURES IN YOUR MIND

Everyone visualizes. Visualizing is the process of creating a mental image. It is something you do many times each day. Visualizing is a natural activity, like breathing or blinking. If you think, you automatically visualize and create images in your mind. Human beings visualize constantly, a process so natural and automatic that most people do not notice when it is occurring.

Everyone Images

The easiest way to illustrate this is to point out that everyone dreams when they sleep. Dreaming is the process of experiencing created images. People also visualize when they daydream. Though the process and the images may seem very similar, dreaming during sleep and daydreaming are not the same.

Images, thoughts, and feelings interact with each other. Your thinking and feeling influence the images you create, and the images you produce can directly affect your thinking and feeling. Regardless of whether you are happy, sad, or angry, the images seen in your mind's eye will express the emotions and thoughts connected to your feelings. For this reason, it's important that you emphasize positive rather than negative images regardless of the type of visualizations you choose to generate.

Making Images

Albert Einstein said, "Imagination is more important than knowledge." He was confirming the belief that visualization plays a primary role in creativity. Mental images are like a flow of thoughts you can see, hear, feel, smell or taste. When you read a book, think about going somewhere, hum a favorite song, call a friend on the phone or do virtually anything mental or physical, your mind visualizes the activity. You spontaneously create images as you read words. You may "see" visual images, or "hear" melodies in response to what you read on a page.

No one knows the exact location where images are produced in the brain, although imaging and visualization are generally considered right-brain activities. While they can seem very real, mental images are quite different from the reality you see with your eyes.

It's the Pictures, Not the Words

Most people don't realize it, but they usually think in images, not words. For instance, when you tell someone you are going to the market, you don't visualize the word, "market," itself. Rather, you spontaneously create a mental image of the structure to which you are going. The word, "market" is a symbol. It represents the image, which is a mental picture of the store as it exists in reality.

Even authors or composers who may be more likely to "hear" rather than see mental images don't visualize in words. The sounds they mentally hear convey the feelings and experience of the object, situation, or melody they are visualizing.

People experience the same process when they think of goals they want to accomplish. Both consciously and unconsciously, a goal and how you plan to achieve it is first "seen" as a visualization. A goal becomes much more attainable when you can purposefully "see" yourself making the goal a reality. Excitement is generated that, in turn, reinforces your desire and drive to accomplish the goal.

Achieving goals brings positive self-images to your mind, while failing to attain them results in negative feelings about yourself. Positive images are experienced as self-enhancing, negative images as failures. When you don't attain a goal, the resulting adverse images often result in lowered self-esteem.

Images

You may be able to generate images in great detail complete with vivid colors, hues, sounds, and textures. It is also possible that you have only a sensation of an image. No matter what your ability to make images, it isn't necessary for you to create highly detailed images in any of the senses to learn and benefit from visualization. Merely having a "feeling" of a mental image, regardless of how clear or dim, is more than enough to do the job.

Your mind creates images in one of two ways: spontaneously, or according to some conscious plan. Spontaneous imagery arises without conscious action or effort. You purposely create some desired image when you have any other visualization.

When you day-dream, images occur in a spontaneous flow through your mind. You don't consciously decide what their form or content will be. In contrast, in an induced visualization you create a specific image to help you remember some piece of information.

Spontaneous Visualization

Spontaneous (or receptive) visualizing is a way of allowing your unconscious mind to speak to your conscious mind. Receptive visualization occurs when you simply allow images to form in your mind's eye. While there may be a specific goal or outcome in mind, you don't consciously determine what the images will be or how long they will stay.

Receptive visualization is helpful for understanding or clarifying problems or issues that you may find confusing, or for revealing your true feelings about a person or situation. Visualizing in a spontaneous fashion helps you expand and explore possibilities.

Spontaneous visualizing can be much like watching a private screening of an unknown movie; you don't know what to expect, and may find yourself surprised and enlightened by the film's message. Often, the images that arise may be vague or blurry, and may require some interpreting for you to understand them.

After years of effort, the scientist, Kekule, suddenly understood the closed nature of Benzine rings and the chemical structure of carbon chains from a visualization he had while dreaming. He imagined a serpent, and saw it roll itself into a circle and grasp its tail in its mouth. The circular theme of the images provided the clue Kekule needed to solve a difficult problem.

Setting future goals is an area in which receptive visualizing can be very helpful. Rather than mentally viewing a pre-arranged program, simply allow a spontaneous flow of images from your unconscious to play across the "picture screen" in your mind.

Open yourself up to possibilities. These are pictures from your unconscious, a visual metaphor of unrealized thoughts and feelings.

Allow the images to flow into your mind in an uncensored and free-floating way. Let your unconscious mind be your ally.

Receptive visualizing can help you identify current barriers that prevent you from doing your best in a particular subject, or on tests in general. Interpreting the images and stories often provides insights into present and future goals. You have a chance of spotting obstacles you might meet along the way.

Programmed Visualization

A kind of reversed communication from Receptive Visualization, Programmed Visualization is a way for your conscious mind to talk to your unconscious mind. Rather than just allowing images to freely form, appear, and disappear as in Spontaneous or Receptive Visualization, you determine what your images will be, how they will appear, and what you will do with them.

You are in charge. You create your visualizations with a predetermined goal in mind. Programmed Visualizing can be especially helpful for you as an aid to overcoming test anxiety and improving your test scores.

Have a specific goal in mind and concentrate on this one area of your life — better study habits, for instance.

❶ Visualize yourself taking the first steps of gathering all the materials you need. See your desk or study area with everything in place and you sitting in a comfortable chair. Image the details, the telephone ringer turned off, door closed, good lighting, etc.

❷ Now visualize yourself taking some deep breaths, relaxing, and getting into a mental frame of mind that encourages studying and learning.

❸ Tell yourself, "I am prepared. I can focus and concentrate. I am able to learn what I need to know." Then, see yourself a week later, studying effectively and confidently as you move from page to page, from book to notes. Observe to yourself, "I am learning what I need to know. The information flows from the page to my mind. I am relaxed and at ease. I am able to study well."

As you accomplish the initial steps in your goal, know that succeeding steps will emerge naturally. Practice what you've imaged. Making it happen will be much easier when you've already seen it in your mind's eye.

Guided Visualization

You're about to experience a technique that combines receptive and programmed imaging to use the best of both modes. Guided Visualization requires that you use your conscious mind to create the scene and most of the details. Your unconscious mind is then free to fill-in what may be missing. The effect is that your conscious and unconscious minds can work together to solve problems and discover solutions.

Guided visualizations are usually created with a goal or end-result in mind. Generally, they are constructed so that you get results in successive steps. Each step closely follows the ones that came before until you achieve your desired goal.

❶ Start by seeing yourself sitting where you normally study. Visualize having everything you need close at hand. Then, image yourself actively going over notes and books. Progress to more involved procedures. See yourself solving the math problems, creating the statistical charts, or drawing the difficult diagrams. In your mind's eye, you are studying effectively. You can feel the work flowing naturally.

❷ Allow your unconscious to add any details it decides are important to make your task easier. Always be aware of giving yourself the chance to be creative, and to see the work from a different perspective. Show yourself new ways to do the job.

❸ To be most effective, the guided visualizations you create must include images of successfully attaining your goal. Imagine yourself relaxed while your study and take tests. "See" yourself getting the good test score. These are the images that help you accomplish whatever you set your sights on.

❹ Review your success images on a daily basis to reinforce them. As confidence in the images grows from deep within, knowing you can succeed becomes more firmly anchored in your mind.

Visualizing and Your Five Senses

There is no right or wrong way to visualize. You visualize in your own unique way. Whatever way you generate images is always the right way. The images you create may be completely non-visual. While humans rely primarily on the sense of sight to visualize, mental images can include any of the five physical senses: sight, sound, touch, taste or smell.

You'd think there would be many words to describe visualizing in the various senses. Unfortunately, the English language offers only one word to describe the process of creating mental images, and that word is visualization.

You can visualize in any number of different ways using your five senses to produce sensory images either in combination or in one sense alone. You may find it easier to create images in one or two senses and more difficult in the others. In any case, visualizations are more real and effective when you can include as many of the five senses as possible.

Visualization and Learning

Very frequently, the sense you use for visualizing is also the sense you most often use for learning. Most people rely primarily on one of their senses when absorbing new information. If you "see" images as most visually oriented people such as designers or artists do, you probably learn and remember the things you see more easily than things you hear, taste, smell or touch.

Musicians usually visualize audibly, and learn and remember what they hear more readily than what they see. According to historical accounts, Mozart, Bach and Beethoven were able to hear melodies that would spontaneously play in their minds.

Athletes learn primarily through their bodies. They express themselves by using bones and muscles to make their statement. As a painter and sculptor, Michelangelo was equally adept at creating both visual and tactile works of art. A wine maker relies heavily upon his impressions of smell and taste in addition to his sense of sight.

Albert Einstein had a vivid imagination. He said he "saw" the solution to a problem long before he formulated the equations that mathematically explained the vision.

Visualizing is powerful because of the intimate interactions that constantly occur between mind and body. Successful athletes use this aspect of visualization to their advantage.

Jean-Claude Killy, winner of three gold medals in the 1972 Winter Olympics, reported that he first skied a course fairly slowly.

As he skied he was memorizing the gates and terrain. He said he experienced this memory both mentally and physically. Once he was out of the starting gate and racing in actual competition, he had no conscious awareness of his movements. He skied automatically, responding to the images of the course he had impressed in his mind/body memory. Based on his winning record in the Olympics and during World Cup competitions, imaging and visualization worked remarkably well for Mr. Killy.

IMPROVING YOUR ABILITY TO VISUALIZE

For many students and people in general, imaging is a long lasting, effective part of any program designed to reduce tension and overcome stress. Imaging is also a major element for improving study habits and performance, finding solutions to difficult personal problems, and defining the goals you want to achieve. It can be a powerful tool for creating positive change in many areas of your life besides studying and test-taking.

While everyone is born with the ability to create images, some are able to visualize much more vividly than others. A person with total recall is said to have a photographic memory and the ability to recreate an eidetic (exact) image of what has been seen. Eidetic images are experienced primarily by elementary school children, with the memory's ability to be photographic fading as the person matures. Most of us don't experience eidetic imagery. However, we are able to create images that are satisfying in our everyday lives.

Like any skill, visualization can be developed and enhanced, or it can be ignored and lost. No matter how good a visualizer you are, the old cliché of "use it or lose it" remains true. As with any skill, if you don't practice and reinforce it, your ability to visualize in any of the five senses will fade. Conversely, the more you visualizing you do, the stronger your skill will become.

Trust Yourself

Visualizing more effectively takes time. It's much like acquiring any skill, except this is a talent most people are born with and then lose because they don't use it in their everyday lives. Creating images requires a certain amount of faith, and the belief that your "visualizing machine" will perform. You must trust the process; image-making operates at an unconscious or preconscious level.

You can't demand that your mind make images any more than you can demand that your body relax. Like relaxation, visualization is more like letting go of something and allowing the images to come to you rather than consciously forcing visualizations to happen.

Regardless of how well you visualize, you can improve. The visualizing exercises that follow build upon your existing talents to create mental images. They are designed to expand your imaging and visualizing abilities. Do them in the order in which they are presented. Each succeeding exercise builds upon the exercises that preceded it.

Don't overlook the value of practice. As with all the techniques described in this book, practice is your best method for learning and improving visualizing skills. Ongoing practice reinforces your visualization experiences and makes the learning more permanent. Improving your visualizing skills will affirm your ability to overcome obstacles and get what you want.

Preparing to Visualize

Effective visualization requires you to be as free from mental and physical tension as is possible. You visualize better when you're relaxed. This is definitely one place where the exercises in relaxation training come into play. The more relaxed your body and mind, the easier it will be for you to create and respond to the images you create.

Rather than attempting to read them from the book, use the CD or a cassette of the visualization exercises. You'll find it's easier to remain fully relaxed when you listen to the recorded scripts. Then you can focus all your awareness on the images in your mind. Relaxing will be very difficult if you have to open your eyes, read each succeeding step, or turn the pages. Getting into the process will be less enjoyable, and not nearly as dynamic.

Relaxing Before Visualizing

Begin your imaging experience by getting comfortable and fully relaxed. Use the exercises that you've found work best for you, or follow the relaxation guide described below. Bring the suggested images to mind and experience each before deciding which ones do the best job. If you find that combining one or more images, or changing an imaging exercise in some way proves more effective for you, go for it!

❶ Lie down, or find a cushioned chair in which to sit, preferably one that leans back and will brace your neck and head. Feel firmly supported so you can smoothly release tension in all the muscles.

❷ Loosen any tight clothing and adjust your body to make yourself as comfortable as possible. To allow easy circulation, uncross your legs, and place your hands at your sides or rest them on your thighs.

❸ Gently close your eyes, and as you do so, notice how your view of reality immediately changes from what goes on outside to what you experience inside. Take a few deep breaths. With each exhale let go of whatever thoughts, concerns, or issues may be occupying your mind at this time. Be calm and at peace. Achieve a state of relaxation in the way you've learned works best for you.

❹ Deepen your state of relaxation in any way you wish. One way is to mentally count backward, very slowly, from twenty to zero. Notice how much more relaxed you become as the numbers get progressively smaller.

If your eyes have not yet closed, you may notice that they are heavier and more difficult to keep open as the numbers approach zero. When they reach zero, you can close your eyes and enjoy the sensations of warmth and heaviness in your arms and legs. Your body is relaxed and comfortable. Now you are ready.

The following exercises are designed to help improve your control over the images you create. Do them in the order in which they are presented. You may breeze right through them all, or you may have to spend some time developing and strengthening your ability in one or more of them. Feel comfortable with your ability to do each exercise before moving on the next. The emphasis should be on developing a strong ability to manipulate the images to fit your needs. This is more important than how crisp or detailed the images or how vivid the color.

Simple Two-Dimensional Object

Draw a picture of a white triangle on a black or dark gray background, or use the one illustrated on the next page. Look directly at the picture for a minute or so, scanning it for details and becoming very familiar with it. Then, close your eyes and imagine the triangle just as you saw it. Allow your mind's eye to slowly scan it as you did when you looked at the real picture. Notice the sharp

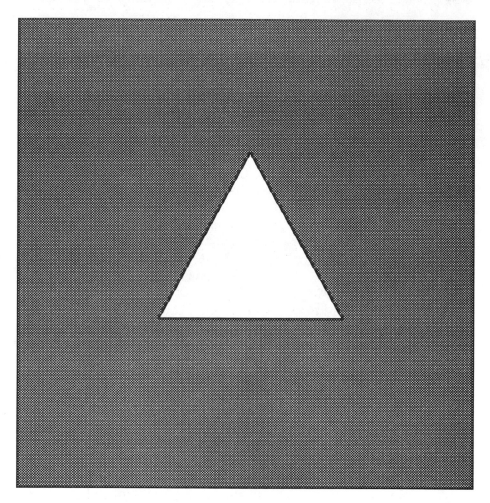

edges and the contrast between the light and dark areas. Try varying the experience. Imagine that the triangle is floating in the air approximately a foot in front of your face. Practice until you are able to visualize and control both the triangle and the background with little or no effort.

The triangle may seem to be an object you are really seeing except that your eyes are closed. It may appear fleetingly, or only a part of it may materialize. You might visualize it for a moment only to have it fade away, or the image could appear as though you were seeing it through a fog or in a darkened room.

None of these experiences means that you can't visualize.

Again, you may not see a sharp or clear image even after doing the exercises a number of times. However, you'll find that as you repeat the exercises the images will become more clear and easier for you to bring to mind. When you become tired or impatient, simply stop.

To repeat, don't force it; you can't "will" visualizations to appear. Now, imagine a white background and make the triangle a color. You can choose any color you wish. When you experience the image to your satisfaction, change the background from white to another color, perhaps a color that contrasts with the color of the triangle. Experiment with the colors. Develop your ability to change them easily and smoothly. Then add textures, from smooth and glassy to rough or knobby. Play with the images; experiment and enjoy.

Simple Three-Dimensional Object

Place a pencil, an orange, or any small, simple object in front of you. Arrange the object with nothing around it and an uncluttered background behind it. Take a few deep breaths, relax, and look directly at the object until you feel you know it. Close your eyes and imagine you still see the object before you. As you look at the object in your mind's eye, scan it just as you did when your eyes were open. Notice its shape and color, the shadows on its surface and any texture or shadings.

Open your eyes and compare your mental image with the object in reality. Note what you missed. Close your eyes and repeat the exercise. It isn't necessary for your image to be an exact match. You want a strong sensory impression. Most people find that with practice, they learn to visualize images more clearly and vividly.

Complex Objects

Now image a more complicated object such as your bicycle, rollerblades, car, a favorite piece of sports equipment, or maybe something purely fanciful or humorous like the strange musician shown on the following page.

Follow the same process described earlier to exercise your imaging muscle. Visualization gives you another valuable tool for learning new material, remembering it, and recalling the information more completely and easily. Besides, it's fun!

Multiple Objects

Go to the drawer in your desk, the one where you store all your loose goodies and valuable junk. Open the drawer and study it for a minute or so. Start at one corner and note the items in sequence as you scan across the drawer. Really notice each object and where it is in relationship to other objects. Note also the different sizes, textures and colors of the various items.

Now close your eyes and visualize the drawer. Start at the same corner as before, and see as many of the items as you can. Then, open your eyes and compare your image with the real thing.

Notice what got left out, altered or misplaced. Close your eyes and fill in the blanks in your mental picture. Each time you create your image, add more details to make it increasingly real. This exercise teaches you that much of what you see gets ignored and forgotten. In reality, people usually focus on only one or two items at a time. As far as the mind is concerned, everything else is out of focus and not worth noticing or remembering.

Picturing Your Room at Home

Here's another imaging exercise that deals with something you probably know quite well. Close your eyes and image your room at home. See yourself standing in the doorway of the room. Slowly scan around the walls until you have "seen" the entire room.

Notice the furniture and the pictures on the walls, the color of the rugs or floor, the bed with its cover and pillows and whether you left your room messy or tidy this morning. See the windows with the sun coming in and the scenery outside. Take in as much of the room as you can. Pay attention to its sights, textures, sounds, smells and anything that feels right to you.

Change your view of the room. See it as though you were at the ceiling. Float around the top of the walls, and see the room from different locations. Now imagine your eye is a camera lens. You are able to zoom in and out to bring details up close or to see the entire room all at once. Next, pick an object in the room and literally see into it. You might even imagine you've become a part of it. Then, focus on the garden outside the window. See the flowers and trees clearly and as close or as far away as you wish. Practice until you can change positions or alter your view in every way imaginable.

Play with the images and discover the extent of your imaging and observing abilities. When you are ready, reorient yourself to reality and open your eyes.

USING YOUR FIVE SENSES

The following visualizations encourage you to image in your five senses. Individually visualizing in each sense lets you become familiar with the ones you've neglected and can now rediscover.

Single Sense Visualizing

This is a way to strengthen your visualizing abilities by focusing on one physical sense at a time. As you do each exercise, you may find distracting thoughts or images in other senses intruding. Without forcing anything, simply let them drift away and refocus on the image in your mind.

To begin, lie down or sit comfortably, take a few deep breaths to help yourself let go and become fully relaxed, and close your eyes. Allow your breathing to become easy and natural.

For this exercise use only *visual images.*

Clear your mind until all you see is black. Now imagine a white triangle on the black background. Notice the perfectly sharp, straight edges of the triangle. Focus on this image for a moment, and then reverse the colors. See a black triangle on a white background.

Let the black triangle become a circle. See the black circle clearly defined on the white background. Change the color of the circle but keep the background white. Let the circle fade away until you see only white. Create a blue square on the white background. Spread the square out to make it a rectangle and change its color to green. Let the rectangle become flatter until all you see is a thin green line. Stretch the line across your field of vision, as though you were pulling an elastic string tighter and tighter. Imagine the string breaking and the ends whipping free.

Allow the images to fade away. Image a crescent moon on a sky blue background. Add twinkling stars. Now play. Create objects in whatever colors you choose, changing the shapes and colors as you wish. Imagine a fantasy of colored stars, planets, and multi-colored comets streaking across the sky. Then, let all images fade away.

Sound

"Whazzat You Say?"

For this exercise, visualize only sounds, not visual images.

Hear the sound of a car horn off in the distance. Notice that it seems to grow louder, as though the car was coming nearer. Then hear the horn as if the car had drawn abreast of you and then begun to move away. Notice how the horn becomes softer and softer as it moves into the distance, until it fades away to silence.

Imagine the sound of a bird chirping. Now hear another bird answering the first. Hear the two birds chirping to each other. Add another bird, and then another, and more until you can hear an entire flock of birds, as though you were standing under a tree full of chirping birds. Let the sound of the birds fade away.

Hear a church bell off in the distance. Its pure ring seems to echo the soft purple of sundown. Listen as the sound gently fades.

Now hear your favorite instrument playing a popular song. Add the sounds of other instruments. Change the music to your favorite song. Play with this sense and visualize any sounds you wish to create in your mind. Then allow your mind to be clear and empty of any sounds.

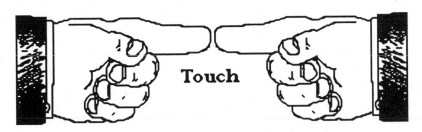

Blindfold your mind's eye and put plugs are in your ears. You cannot see or hear. Experience only tactile feelings while doing the following exercises.

You are sitting on a hardwood floor. Feel the firm coolness through your clothing and against your legs and buttocks. As your hands explore the floor you can feel the texture of the wood and the edges between one wood piece and the next. Your hand encounters something hard and round, smooth, cold and quite small. It fits in the palm of your hand and you decide it is a marble. Next to it is a soft, fuzzy, flexible thing that is also round: a smerf ball. Notice the differences in touch that range from hard, smooth, cold and small to soft, warm and fuzzy.

Something rubs against your leg. You reach over to find a small, warm, and furry creature. Your hands tell you this little bundle of activity is a young puppy. You pick it up and put it in your lap. Pet it gently and scratch behind its ears. Feel the soft fur and warm body. Then feel its warm and wet tongue as it licks your hand and face. Roll it over in your lap and stroke the puppy's soft tummy. Allow the image to fade away.

Now you're sitting outside on cool grass. The sun is shining, warm on your arms and face. A soft breeze begins to stir, and you can feel its coolness on your skin. Enjoy these sensations and any others you wish to experience. Then, allow your mind to become blank and still. Focus on your relaxation.

Smell

Turn off all the other senses, and allow your imagination to focus solely on your olfactory receptor.

Concentrate on odors you have experienced. The nose with its sense of smell is the most sensitive receptive organ in humans and most animals. Yet, it is the imaginative sense that people most easily forget and lose. We don't need to place as much importance on the sense of smell as do animals, and through lack of use we lose an entire world of enjoyment.

Fully experience each odor or fragrance before allowing it to fade from your consciousness. Imagine you've passed the door to a bakery. The odor of freshly baked bread, fragrant and inviting, warm from the oven wafts past your nostrils. Let the image slowly fade. Now imagine the sensual scent of freshly cut roses.

Bring other odors to mind, perhaps your favorite food or perfume. Experiment with unpleasant odors, like the smell of tar or the exhaust fumes from a bus. If you have ever encountered the defensive end of a skunk, you will have no trouble bringing that particularly pungent smell to mind. Build your skills by switching odors quickly. Visualize similar yet subtly different odors such as the fragrances of different flowers or fruit. Then, put your nose to sleep.

Shut off all other senses and activate your imaginary taste buds.

Salivating as you do the exercises is a good sign your imaging is both active and accurate. Be sure you allow each image to fade completely before moving on to the next.

First, create the image of a sugar cube slowly melting on your tongue and releasing its sweetness to your mouth and taste-buds. Follow the sweet, sugar taste on your tongue and back into your throat. Allow that sensation to fade. Then, bring to mind the image of salt, intense and sharp.

Note the contrast between the sweetness of sugar and the sharpness of the salt. Imagine the taste of a juicy orange, fresh, sweet and cool. Experience it washing away the salty taste. Switch to the rich flavor of your favorite cake or pastry. Follow with the sensations of a steaming cup of coffee or tea. Cool your mouth with the delicious taste of your favorite ice cream. Top the ice cream with chocolate drops, sprinkles, gummy bears, or anything you would enjoy. Experiment with different tastes. Give yourself the pleasure of sampling different flavors, textures and temperatures.

Allow the sensations to fade and rest quietly for a moment. Which senses were the most real and vivid for you? Is the sense in which you visualize best also the one you use for learning?

Combining All the Senses

Now for a visualization that incorporates all your five senses. As each action and sensation is described, see and feel it in as many ways as you can with your body as well as your mind. Make the experience complete and vivid.

Begin by seeing yourself in a kitchen. You are standing at the counter in front of a large assortment of fresh fruit. It can be any kitchen with which you are familiar, and any kind of fruit. Reach for a piece of fruit that you like. Imagine the fruit clearly. See the variations in color and texture, feel its shape. Is it round like an orange, shaped like an apple, or curved and thick like a banana?

Notice the skin. Feel whether it is apple smooth or textured like an orange. Lift it up in the palm of your hand and feel its weight. If it needs to be peeled, do that now. Dig your thumbs into it or grasp the skin and draw it down. See the inner flesh appear as you pull the skin away. Note how the color of the inside skin contrasts with the outside. Enjoy the inviting odor, and notice when your mouth begins to water.

Lift the piece of fruit toward your face and take your first bite. Savor the delicious flavor that floods your mouth as you enjoy the taste of the fruit. Chew the bite of fruit slowly and feel yourself swallow. See yourself eating the entire piece of fruit, piece by piece and bite by bite.

Allow all your senses to be active and make the experience as real and as enjoyable as possible. When you finish eating, see yourself washing your hands in the kitchen sink and then drying them. Pause for a moment's reflection on your experience, and allow the image to fade from your mind. Gently open your eyes.

CREATING A SAFE PLACE

Why should you create an image of a safe place? What can it do to improve your concentration, reduce those anxious feelings and improve your grades? A lot, as it turns out.

Students report an automatic association with an internal safe place and deep relaxation. When excessive anxiety rears its ugly head, a quick trip to your safe place becomes a shortcut to relieving the anxious feelings and regaining a sense of calm.

With practice, merely bringing this special place to mind relieves your tension. It's the same feeling of relief as when you arrive at the airport early, instead of being late and frantically rushing while you worry about missing the plane.

Your safe place is an inner haven from anxiety and stress. Once

established, a safe place becomes a barrier to outside distractions as well as an inner sanctuary. You create a mental bubble where you are "in" and everything and everybody else is "out." You can study and take tests with greater focus when you are within a safe place.

A safe place is one where outsiders cannot intrude or interfere, and where you can feel safe and secure, at peace and comfortable. Your safe place begins with relaxation, so it's a great image to bring to mind before beginning to study or when you prepare for a test.

When you're in the middle of a test and begin to feel too anxious, take a brief moment to bring your safe place to mind and you'll feel calmed and reassured. However, quickly achieving a safe place does take practice.

A safe inner place can be anywhere or have any appearance you choose. It might be outdoors at the seashore or the mountains, or perhaps a beautiful meadow with a softly bubbling stream that meanders beneath overhanging trees. It can be indoors, and take the form of a study, den, cabin, or your own bedroom.

Your safe place can be based on reality, such as a place you've visited or read about, or it can be purely imaginative, a unique product of your own originality and creativity. Chances are, it will be a combination of both real and imaginary. Most importantly, it should bring with it a sense of well-being, peace, and safety.

Everything in this special place is within your power and control. There are no limitations on what you can safely do or experience.

You can add or remove anything you wish at any time. You will use this special, safe place in many ways. It's an inner retreat where you can go to relieve tension, solve problems, make decisions, or to simply "get away from it all."

For these reasons, your safe place needs to be both inviting and comfortable. You might include room for lying down and perhaps a cozy recliner for sitting and relaxing. This is also a place to go to when you want a brief escape from current pressures and to not think at all.

Experiencing Your Safe Place

To create a safe place, begin by achieving a state of deep relaxation. Notice the images that form and flow across your mental viewing screen. Ask yourself what image would represent a safe place. Then, let your mind go deep inside. Give your imagination the freedom to create an answer.

For example, you might imagine a castle with strong, thick, tall walls to resist outside invasion or intrusion, complete with a moat and drawbridge. Inside the castle proper, you can go down a flight of stairs to an even more secure area. Your safe place could be a room at the bottom of the staircase, buried deep within the castle.

It could also be a room at the top of a tall tower, with large windows so you can see the surrounding area. Perhaps you envision a secluded harbor on a lush tropical island. The possibilities are unlimited and whatever you choose to imagine is perfectly fine.

Once you've established a safe place, take the time to explore your inner haven and to discover its unique features. Return to it often. The repetition will reinforce the images and make access easier and more automatic.

IMAGES FOR PERSONAL PROBLEM SOLVING

When personal problems are filling your mind and clouding your thinking, it's very difficult to concentrate clearly on school issues. You need to have a clear mind for studying and test-taking. To begin, make yourself comfortable and bring the image of your special place to mind.

When you are comfortably ready, think of the current problem. With no external interference to cause distractions, you can review the problem and work it through in a more calm and relaxed state of mind. As you mull it over, you may find yourself with a fresh view. Perhaps you'll see facets or meanings and come up with novel solutions that surprise you.

The following visual metaphors present different approaches to problem solving, both personal and academic. They are designed to facilitate your imagination and tap into your own, unique, creative potential. Try each of them to see which helps you find the most effective solutions to the problem you are facing.

❶ Imagine you are in an elevator that is slowly descending. As it goes down you can go deeper into understanding your problem. When you are ready, the elevator can stop and the doors will open onto a possible answer. You can accept this solution or continue to go downward. Each time the elevator stops the doors will open onto another solution. In addition, as the elevator descends lower, you can find yourself becoming more and more deeply relaxed.

❷ In front of you is a large basket of fortune cookies. Each cookie contains a possible solution to the problem you are facing. No matter how many fortune cookies you open, each solution will be different and the basket will never run out of cookies.

❸ You are sitting in a chair with a ventriloquist's dummy on your lap. You describe the problem to the dummy and it begins to talk back to you, giving you suggestions and possible solutions. This dummy doesn't need for you to pull its strings. It hears the problem and reveals new insights each time it opens its mouth. It's a very smart dummy.

❹ Imagine yourself at a carnival, standing in front of the Wheel-Of-Fortune. You spin the wheel. Each time it comes to a stop the wheel reveals another possible answer to your problem. No matter how many times you spin the wheel it will expose another solution, or a part of the best solution to the problem.

❺ You are in a large room. An unassembled jigsaw puzzle lies on the carpeted floor. All the pieces are face down. With your problem in mind, begin to turn the puzzle pieces over. Notice that each piece represents part of an answer to the problem you wish to solve. You can turn over and fit together any number of pieces until you have a clear understanding of the problem and its solution.

❻ A deck of cards lies face-down before you. Rather than the usual red and black, diamonds, spades, clubs or hearts, the face of each card is a different full-colored picture. As you turn the cards over and place them next to each other, the complete picture of a solution to your problem takes shape. Many pictures and solutions are possible

❼ If you really find yourself "boxed in" by a problem, just go with it. Imagine yourself inside the locked box that represents your problem. Visualize how you would react. The images that come to you can help your understanding of what is blocking your progress. In virtually all cases, the solutions to problems reside within you; it's a matter of releasing the answer to your conscious mind.

IMAGING FOR DEEP RELAXATION

The following scripts are especially useful before studying or going to sleep. Suggestions added at the end of the script can either energize you or enervate you. It is particularly helpful to listen to the scripts with a CD or audio tape player that shuts itself off automatically.

The exercises are almost impossible to do if you must continually look at the book. they are very effective if you can simply lie back, close your eyes, and follow the sound of the voice.

❶ Visualize a very thick, heavy, twisted rope, such as the kind used to tie a ship to the dock. Imagine the rope going from taut to slack. See one end of the rope as it begins to slowly untwist and unravel. Notice how the individual strands unwind from each other. The strands slowly separate and uncurl, the fibers becoming straight and loose. Your anxious feelings and the rope can unravel together. As the rope strands unravel in your imagination, feel any twists and kinks unravel from your muscles. Feel tension in your mind unravelling at the same time.

❷ In your mind's eye, imagine a large block of ice. It is in the bright sun and you can see the ice beginning to melt. Notice the pools of water that gather at the bottom of the block. You can see them forming little rivulets that flow away from the block of ice.

Feel the tension draining away with the slow trickle of the water making tracks down the block of ice. Watch the watery trails of the melting ice, and experience excess tension melting out of you.

❸ Visualize a smooth, glassy pond. See a pebble fall into the water, and watch it create small waves that subside into ripples. Notice how the waves turn into smaller and smaller ripples as they spread outward from the spot where the pebble entered the water.

In your imagination, follow the pebble as it slowly sinks to the bottom of the pond. See the water beneath the surface regain its calmness. Continue to watch until the water in the pond is glassy smooth once again. Notice your body letting go. Feel your muscles becoming warmer and more flexible as the ripples in the water become smaller and smaller, and finally disappear.

❹ Imagine you are in a warm bath, one where the water stays at just the right temperature. Feel the action of the calming water on your body, releasing tension and bringing comfort. Notice how easily the soothing warmth penetrates deep into muscles and bones, loosening tension and restoring vitality and feelings of well-being. You can experience yourself becoming more and more deeply relaxed in both mind and body.

Use your imagination to come up with other visualizing metaphors that encourage you to release tension and invite relaxation. For your imagination, there are no limits.

SUMMING UP

Use your imagination. Learn to let it run freely. Have fun creating your own images for relaxation, studying, test-taking or whatever. As you release unnecessary tension and reach a state of relaxation and ease, you might decide this is a good time to become even more completely focused and in touch with your inner abilities. A proven way to do that is through an even deeper state of relaxation. That is the subject of Step 4: Using auto-hypnosis.

Step 4: IMPROVING FOCUS AND CONCENTRATION

Using Hypnosis

"You don't know all the things you can do. You can use hypnosis to explore, knowing you are going to find something that you don't know about yet."

Milton H. Erickson, M.D.

ABOUT AUTO-HYPNOSIS

Remember a warm spring day when you were sitting in a class at school. You gazed out the window at green grass, bright flowers and shady trees. You really didn't see them because you were lost in a daydream. Suddenly you realized the class was over and you had no clue what the teacher had said or how much time had passed. You didn't know what had happened.

All your attention was on the image in your mind. During your daydream, the teacher's voice became a distant drone. Things happening around you that would normally be at the center of your awareness became unimportant. The visual image in your mind, the daydream, had become the focus of your complete concentration. Without realizing it and with no effort at all, you had slipped into a state of auto-hypnosis.

Clearly, a major part of auto-hypnosis is about focusing your attention on a single idea or image while tuning out distractions. Some define it as an altered state of consciousness and a different way of being or thinking. Others believe auto-hypnosis occurs when an individual uses normal mental processes in a special way. Regardless of how we define it, there really is no mystery about how people accomplish a state of auto-hypnosis. They do it naturally and effortlessly.

What It Does for You

Auto-hypnosis is an easily learned skill. It allows you to give yourself goal-directed suggestions to improve study skills, focus more completely, take tests more calmly, and block negative self-statements. Since the very nature of auto-hypnosis is a centering of your focus, energy and attention, it is a superb tool for improving your concentration. That will be its primary value for you. This chapter helps you acquire the skills so you can put yourself into a meditative or hypnotic state quickly and easily.

Trance is Natural

Just as when you visualize, focusing on one thing at a time is something you do naturally, every day of your life. Because you can tune out the other hundreds of things in your surroundings that simultaneously vie for your attention, you are able to accomplish many things such as reading, listening to music, playing sports, cooking a great dish, or accomplishing the many different tasks that make up your day.

Can you imagine what life would be like if you couldn't choose which specific things you wished to pay attention to at any moment? You would be physically and emotionally paralyzed and unable to function. Your experience of life would be the same as that of an autistic person or some schizophrenics, continually bombarded by an endless and assaulting stream of sights and sounds from their surroundings.

They are unable to fine tune their attention or focus on any one thing. With so much going on at the same time, they can find no way to make sense of the world in which they live and sometimes become hypersensitive to light, noise and touch. Such individuals will often retreat into fantasy because they have no sense of control over the reality of their lives.

What It's Not and What It Is

Auto-hypnosis is not something that one person does to another. Forget the Hollywood image of some sinister person swinging a bright medallion before your eyes and saying, "You are in my power." You definitely do not give control of your feelings, thoughts, or actions to someone else. No one can force or coerce you into a hypnotic state; you allow yourself to enter into it.

Hypnosis is an intentional process. You enter into a trance because you want to, which means that virtually all hypnosis is self-hypnosis. With few exceptions, the process is not the popular myth found in books, movies, television or the theater.

It may be hard to believe, but most people experience a number of light trances every day as they focus on one task or another. That's not the same as purposefully putting yourself into a state of hypnosis. Any time you focus intently on something and tune out everything else, you are essentially in trance.

If you are skeptical that you can become hypnotized or don't believe it is a voluntary act, I encourage you to remain skeptical. Then, when you follow a script and have an unusual and pleasing experience, you will be the first to know that something different has occurred.

Basic Skills

In order to purposely put yourself into a hypnotic trance, you must first learn a few essential skills.

Skill Number ❶ is to establish a comfortable place in which to practice and experience. Preferably, this should be a place that is quiet and free from distractions. Turn off the phone, dim the lights, and settle back in a comfortable chair that will support your head, neck and back. Eliminate any gum, loosen any tight clothing, and remove your eyeglasses or contact lenses. Taking out your contact lenses is especially important; very often during meditative or hypnotic states your eyes can become a bit dry.

Skill Number ❷ is on-demand relaxation. By this time you know very well how to "let go," and to achieve deep relaxation. You realize that being truly relaxed means letting go of excess tension.

You must also be willing to put aside any distracting thoughts or concerns during your relaxation period. Besides relaxation, "letting go" means being willing to discover and experience the new and different. It also means giving up any preconceived notions you may have about auto-hypnosis and its effects. This is a time to play, to explore new sensations, and to let your imagination be creative and alive.

Skill Number ❸ is simply allowing something to happen. Auto-hypnosis is not a job or an assignment. You don't achieve an hypnotic state by "trying."

To begin with, "trying" is already what you have done a lot of: you've tried not to worry, spent time trying to study effectively, tried to do better on tests. "Trying" has not been an effective solution. In fact, "trying" has probably become part of the problem. After all, the more you try and don't succeed, the more convinced you become that you'll will never do better. The result is that "trying" becomes more connected with failure than with success.

Furthermore, "trying" splits your attention and nullifies your efforts. It implies that if you work very hard and expend a great deal of energy and perspiration, you can force something to happen. "Trying" is the opposite of "allowing." The emphasis on all the exercises you experience in this chapter, and in the entire book, is to simply let a natural process develop and expand. Don't attempt to force anything to happen.

Skill Number ❹ is connecting suggestions with images. Suggestions are the bridge between your normal state of consciousness and a state of auto-hypnosis. Whether the suggestions come from you as an internal dialogue, a CD or audio tape you listen to, or through the voice of someone speaking to you, they form the platform on which you build images in your mind.

It's much like a printed novel. The words on the page are symbols. They become translated by your mind into images. A gripping story is one that you really "get into." It holds you by the vividness of the images you create as you read the words on the page. In a sense, you live the narrative. You experience emotions such as excitement, sadness, fright or pleasure as the tale unfolds.

Still, they are just words, ink laid on paper. What is truly remarkable is how your mind creates those graphic images from the hieroglyphics you see printed on the page. In the same way, mental images formed from the suggestions you hear are the key to successfully entering and using auto-hypnosis.

Skill Number ❺ is exercising the freedom to improvise and substitute. If the auto-hypnosis scripts and suggestions that follow are not to your liking, feel free to either modify them or create your own from scratch. Don't hesitate to alter suggestions in any way that will make them do the job better, and to change or eliminate those that don't work.

For example, a fear of water is almost guaranteed to make you anxious whenever you hear suggestions to create images of being in a boat, swimming, floating, lakes, the ocean or any body of water. These types of images will either make it difficult for you to enter into hypnosis, or will cause you to bring yourself out of your meditative or trance state.

Skill Number ❻ is giving up any expectations of "doing it right." No two people are exactly the same, and no two people will enter into or experience an auto-hypnotic state the same way. They will not go to the same depth of relaxation, or know the same sensations while in trance. What is right for someone else may be wrong for you, and vice versa.

Tom found that specific images, regardless of the subject, didn't do the job at all. For him, drifting comfortably in an all encompassing lavender haze or cloud is what did the trick. He explained that there were no visible boundaries or limitations, and this gave him the freedom to accept and act upon suggestions without hesitation or doubts. Janice found that imagining herself in the black expanse of outer space achieved the same results.

Very simply, there is no "right" or "wrong" way to do hypnosis. However you experience it is perfectly fine. It's your mind and body, your imagination, and your comfort that counts. Make your experiences with auto-hypnosis meaningful, appropriate, and satisfying. As you strengthen your ability to achieve auto-hypnosis and gain confidence, you'll learn how to enter an hypnotic state more quickly and reach deeper levels. You'll maintain the level that works best, and easily bring yourself out of trance to full mental alertness.

Use All Your Senses

You enhance your suggestions by using all the physical senses you can, just as you did with the visualization exercises in Step 3.

If the suggestion is that you imagine yourself stepping onto an escalator and moving downward, really "see" yourself and "feel" yourself experiencing the sensations as you step onto the moving stairway. Notice the feelings as your hand finds and grasps the handrail, and the sensations of movement under your feet. Observe your body's reactions as the escalator with you standing on it travel to progressively lower levels.

The visual and physical sensations need not be as vivid as those described above. The important part of making auto-hypnosis an effective tool is being fully involved. Just as with the visualization exercises, it isn't necessary to have clear and precise images when you visualize. It is enough to have an idea or "sense" of the images and be able to manipulate them. The sensations and movement in your body will bring the experiences to life for you.

AUTO-HYPNOSIS: DIFFERENT USES

Although you're learning this new skill as part of a program to lessen or overcome test anxiety, hypnosis has proven dramatically effective in many areas. In the field of medicine, hypnosis is used to minimize pain during and after surgical and dental procedures. It promotes quicker healing after injury or surgery, helps to relieve asthma symptoms, and so on. It isn't a medical panacea, but where it is applicable, a ton of research proves it definitely works.

Certainly, the real value of auto-hypnosis for you is how easy and useful it is for anxiety relief and improving your studying and grades. You can also use it in other areas of your life. Helping yourself gently drift off to sleep is one example. After putting yourself into trance, give yourself the suggestion that you will fall asleep effortlessly, sleep soundly, and awaken refreshed and rested.

Caroline found she could eliminate the "afternoon-blahs" by establishing a light, auto-hypnotic trance. She then suggested to herself that a five minute relaxation would feel as though she'd just had a long, energizing rest. Caroline aroused herself feeling re-energized and without the groggy feeling that often follows an afternoon nap.

Auto-hypnosis is very useful for active-relaxation as well. This is when you actively engage in work, study, play, or whatever, and suggest to yourself that you are calm and at ease, peaceful, confident and fully focused. You can maintain these feelings as you accomplish your project or task.

Rick is a student at UCLA. He learned to create a mental work space in which to study and take tests. It didn't matter where he really was; by putting himself into an hypnotic state, Rick created his own zone where virtually nothing bothered or distracted him. He found he could use this zone anywhere, and while doing many of his usual activities.

Athletes have long used auto-hypnosis to improve performance. A professional golfer learned to put himself into a state of hypnosis as he stood over the ball. Once there, he created a tunnel of vision so that everything outside his view of the ball was out of focus and unimportant. As he concentrated on the ball, it became even more sharply defined and appeared to be larger. He found he could hit it more cleanly and with greater accuracy.

A number of books focus on improving your tennis game. They suggest you focus all your mental energy on the ball and allow your body simply to do what comes naturally. Runners strain to reach a certain "high" that some have described as "an out of body experience where you can't feel your feet hitting the ground and you don't run out of energy." Professional athletes and, indeed, entire teams often use auto-hypnosis to achieve their highest level of performance and endurance.

THE NATURE OF SUGGESTIONS

Suggestions are your way of communicating what you consciously want to accomplish to your unconscious mind. Your unconscious mind then puts the suggestions into action. Suggestions are most effective when you make them in an auto-meditative frame of mind. That is the part of auto-hypnosis that occurs after the induction when you've begun to meditate deeply. It is during this phase that your unconscious is most ready to hear and accept the suggestions made to it.

Make Them Positive

Always create suggestions using positive wording, and direct them to the specific goals you wish to achieve. At the same time, they should also address the feelings you want to have about yourself. For instance, telling yourself "I will try not to be worried about tests" is a weak suggestion because it implies a distinct possibility of failure. It doesn't deal with the real issue, which is your anxiety about studying and testing.

A more effective and positive way to word a suggestion is, "Each day I find myself more and more comfortable as I study for my upcoming test," or, "I am able to concentrate and focus more completely each time I sit down to study." These statements are positive and empowering. They predict success.

Make Them Powerful

Suggestions have more power when they address a number of purposes that are all directed toward the same goal. Note that each of the suggestions made above is quite general, yet each relates to both an immediate goal and the overall desire for an improved self-image. Most suggestions are directed primarily at actions and attitudes. When worded well, they can be very empowering. The key is to word your suggestions with self-empowerment in mind. Then you help your unconscious promote new ways of looking at events and circumstances. You'll experience a positive attitude and a sense of power over whatever task or problem you encounter.

Suggestions are usually made when you want to do, or not do something. In either case you have some desired outcome in mind. Not-doing something is actually the more important first step if you want to change a self-defeating behavior or belief.

Start by coupling the not-to-do part with a positive statement. This encourages change in both actions and attitudes at the same time. For instance: "I choose to not become upset, and to remain calm and at ease. I'll cope with this coming exam to the best of my ability. I will continue on my schedule, still calm and peaceful."

Another example is, "I can be relaxed and feel more and more secure in my abilities. I choose to not allow my mind to wander. I can be fully attentive, and focused on the task at hand." One last example to consider, "I am strong and capable. During tests my mind can remain clear, calm, and fully in charge. Everything I need to know can come to me as I need it."

Notice that the examples do not state that an action or feeling *will* occur. Instead, each suggests that it *can* happen, particularly when you choose to *have* it happen.

Make Them Fit for You

Whatever your suggestion, it must feel "right" to you. Statements that come only from your head don't have much energy or "push" behind them. Avoid making global statements or stating goals where there's a slim possibility of success. Suggestions that cover too much territory, too soon, are usually unattainable. You'll find yourself resisting them and that is definitely not what you want to have happen. Suggestions work best when you keep them simple and pointed to a clearly defined goal.

No matter how well a suggestion is worded or how good it feels, it probably will not immediately alter a firmly established attitude or course of action. Change takes a while; give your suggestions a reasonable period of time to work.

EXPERIENCING AUTO-HYPNOSIS

The following two scripts introduce you to the experience of hypnotic trance. They both incorporate all the techniques you've previously learned about breathing, physical relaxation and visualization. You may find yourself able to "get into" one script more than the other, or they may prove equally effective. Regardless of which script you use, allow yourself to become fully absorbed in the flow of words. The more involved and focused your attention is, the more vague and unimportant everything around you will become.

When you are in a hypnotic state, the world outside your conscious awareness is unimportant. It should offer no competition to your concentration. This is precisely what can occur when you study or take a test. You want to focus completely on the subject in front of you. You don't want to be disturbed by anything that would interfere when you're studying or taking a test.

Creating a Helpful Habit

Another goal of these first scripts is to help you develop a certain habit or expectation about hypnosis, a type of meditative frame of mind. This is a different mind-set than the one you use during your everyday activities. A well-known actor described it as undergoing a distinct mental shift. He immersed himself in a role completely, and found that his attention shifted from the outer world as he usually knew it to the imaginary world defined by the screenwriter. When he worked, he literally forgot the real world and concentrated only on the world inhabited by his character.

It's developing a meditative frame of mind that makes auto-hypnosis easy and effective to use. A group of students attending a class experienced this frame of mind in another way. After attending a few of the classes and entering into auto-hypnosis on each occasion, they found they would spontaneously go into a meditative state upon entering the classroom. Because they were mentally tuned-in to the upcoming class, simply passing through the doorway triggered a shift from their ordinary external reality to a very different internal one.

FIRST HYPNOTIC EXPERIENCES

It's time for you to experience auto-hypnosis for yourself. As you listen to the voice on the CD or cassette offering suggestions, simply go with the images that flow into your mind. Don't analyze or "think" about what you hear or experience. There will be plenty of time for that after you've completed the exercise.

Every hypnosis session lasts for a specific time. Like a story, it has a beginning, a middle, and an end. You can't get lost or "stuck" in a hypnotic state, so it's fine to let go and leave the ordinary world for a brief time. If you go too deep or get too comfortable, you'll simply drift off to sleep and awaken feeling very refreshed.

I encourage you to experience both hypnosis scripts. The Balloon script is on the CD, while one of the other professionally made CDs or audio tapes includes both scripts. You can make your own audio tape by reading the scripts directly from this book.

When you're ready, turn on the CD or tape player. Make yourself comfortable. Simply do as the recorded voice suggests. Experience auto-hypnosis using one or both of the scripts, before attempting to enter trance on your own.

You're In Control

You can feel comfortable and safe as you enter an inner world where you are in complete control. You decide how long you will remain in trance and how deep you will go. You decide what the focus will be. In short, you have complete discretion of your actions while experiencing hypnosis.

Knowing you can satisfactorily achieve deep hypnosis is an important step in your program. You'll use this skill to minimize your test anxiety and improve your test scores. Get ready to listen, and to experience...

Balloons

"I'm making myself comfortable in a reclining chair or couch. My head and neck are supported and my body is at ease... my arms at my sides, hands resting on my thighs... I know I don't have to "try" to do anything... that I can simply allow something to happen... and I can go with it."

"I find a spot on the wall across from me. I look comfortably at this spot and focus my complete attention on it... as I stare at the spot I take in a deep breath of air and expand my lungs as fully as I can... holding the air for a moment... and as I breathe out I hear my inner signal to let go in my mind... and continuing to focus on that spot..."

"I breathe deeply two or three more times... each time giving myself the inner signal as I exhale... to let go... (wait 60 seconds) allowing my breathing to slow... becoming slow and gentle... even... and regular... no effort at all... breathing naturally... noticing that the spot seems to be changing... becoming softer... fuzzier... foggy... harder to keep in sharp focus as my eyes become more and more tired... and they may have a tendency to blink..."

"I wonder to myself, will my eyes close all at once...or flutter a bit first as some parts of my body begin to experience the comfort of deep relaxation and auto-hypnosis... how soon will I forget about my heavy eyes... and begin letting the rest of my body settle more deeply into the chair... and become even more comfortable... with every breath I take, with every minute that passes... more comfortable and more deeply relaxed... eyelids are very heavy now... wanting to close... I don't have to move or make any sort of effort... don't even have to hold my eyes open..."

"It will be interesting... to experience that moment... when I can no longer hold them open... beginning to close... or they may have already closed... I feel the supporting comfort deepening... drifting... my eyes remain closed... so comfortable I would rather not even try to open them...

"More relaxed and at ease... recognizing that I don't have to move, talk, or let anything bother me... because there is nothing really important except the activity of my unconscious mind, and that can be whatever my unconscious mind desires... and it really doesn't matter what my conscious mind does because my unconscious mind automatically will do just what it needs to... to help me achieve what it is I desire... drifting... listening to my voice and letting go... relaxing... feeling heavier as my body settles even more deeply into comfortable relaxation..."

"Drifting with my voice... comfortable, yet in control... knowing I can always be aware of what needs to be noticed... that a part of my mind hears the words... can respond when I need to... that I can arouse myself whenever I want to... this is so comfortable, so easy to drift deeper and deeper... with no need to pay attention to my physical comfort... less and less important to pay attention to my voice... some part of my mind will hear it for me... "

"These feelings of comfort and relaxation seem to occur even more rapidly... and I can experience, more and more, any kind of sensation I wish... I've learned to recognize many of my body sensations... warm... cold... muscle tension... relaxation..."

"Drifting... more and more completely at ease... nothing to bother me... nothing to disturb me... seeing images drifting across the screen in my mind... in the place in my mind that makes pictures... like leaves on a gentle stream, floating into view and then floating out of sight... just letting the images flow through my mind... sharp images... hazy pictures... colors..."

"Not really paying attention, just letting something happen... allowing myself to drift... ready now for more... wanting more... relaxed and in control... ready to go into deep relaxation and experience auto-hypnosis for myself..."

"Very easy, very pleasant, very natural... ready to go deeper... bringing an image to mind... seeing an escalator in my mind's eye... an escalator that goes downward... knowing that I can step onto the escalator and travel downward... see myself and feel myself as I step onto the escalator... easily and automatically... without effort... without hesitation... going downward to the level that is right for me... today... at this time... each level down taking me deeper and deeper... comfortably... naturally... going down... past the first level... relaxing even more... down... level two... feeling more and more relaxed... feeling more and more a part of the image... experiencing the feelings of going deeper and deeper.."

"Third level... deeper with every breath I take.... deeper with every minute that passes... fourth level and traveling down to the level I know is right for me... just letting go and going deeper... and now the fifth level, drifting deeper... nothing to bother or disturb... and finally, stepping off the escalator... at the right level..".

"Noticing how this feels so I can remember these sensations... experiencing the feelings of deep relaxation... the feelings of auto-hypnosis... of deepening hypnosis... stepping off the escalator is like coming to a new place... like leaving the everyday world behind... leaving cares and concerns behind... and entering into a very special and safe place... a calm place... peaceful..."

"My body is resting comfortably... supported... secure... my arms lying comfortably by my sides... hands on my thighs... feeling the fabric under my fingers and against my palms..."

"Images forming in my mind... images of looking at my right hand... seeing a string tied around the wrist... following the string upward to find that it's tied to many big, round, brightly colored balloons... all of them my favorite colors... or maybe one favorite color... all filled with helium... light... floating at the end of the strings... just floating, so light and easy... tugging up toward the sky... effortless... focusing on how light and airy they are... floating upward... noticing the tug where they're tied to the wrist..".

"Noticing the hand beginning to feel light, just like the balloons... wondering how soon one of the fingers may begin to feel especially light... may begin to lift up... noticing which finger begins to move... and wondering which finger will move next... seeing the balloons reaching for the sky... feeling the tug on the string... the fingers becoming lighter... the whole hand becoming lighter..."

"Focusing on the feelings of lightness in the fingers, the hand... as it begins to lift... and it feels even lighter... becoming lighter and lighter as it slowly lifts... the higher it lifts, the lighter it feels... the lighter it feels, the higher it goes... floating... all by itself... drifting higher and lighter... lighter and higher... the balloons lifting...

lighter... higher...the elbow bending and the arm lifting even higher... effortless... easily... comfortable... relaxed... comfortable and relaxed all over... the hand and arm floating with the balloons... without effort... just hanging in the air like the balloons..".

"And then... watching the string as it slowly comes untied... falling from the wrist... the balloons floating higher, away from me... higher and higher... up into the sky... becoming smaller and smaller... and the arm begins to slowly come down... slowly... gently back down... body becoming more relaxed as the arm lowers... down... down to a comfortable resting place by my side... knowing that when the arm touches my thigh or the chair... I will be even more relaxed... and into a deep state of hypnosis... now..."

"In this deep state of hypnosis... without realizing it... many things have changed in my body... my rate of breathing... my pulse ... blood pressure... I have no desire to move.. and I can remain comfortably immobile... until it's time to move... recognizing how very well I've done... how easily I've achieved a state of hypnosis... acquired a new skill... how comfortable and enjoyable a trance can be... just imagining what hypnosis can help me to accomplish..."

"The mind is so complex... I can go into a hypnotic state to find out a whole lot of things I can do... and they are so many more than I ever dreamed of... abilities I don't yet know about... abilities that can be expressed in deep hypnosis... I feel hopeful... I've done something new... mastered self-auto-hypnosis... I can accomplish my goals... master the subjects... overcome test anxiety... focus and concentrate completely... as I'm doing now... at this moment... feeling I can accomplish whatever I want to... willing and eager to show myself what I am capable of doing..."

"And now... it's time to awaken... easy to do... no effort at all... to come back to full awareness... and I don't have to lose these comfortable feelings... or what my unconscious mind has learned... and when my unconscious knows... I can return again to this comfortable state... and learn more... so I can accomplish more... I can go back to the escalator... step on, and begin to go up... upward toward the top level... up toward being alert and aware... and as I ride up the escalator I can find myself beginning to awaken... easily... knowing that when I reach the second level my eyes will open... when I reach the top I'll feel refreshed and alert... mind fully aware... and I can keep the feelings of being comfortable and at ease... refreshed... alert... completely and fully awake... and feeling wonderful!" (End of Script)

The Staircase

"I make myself comfortable and at ease... adjusting myself to the most relaxing position... my head, neck and body are gently supported... I feel ready to experience deep relaxation and auto-hypnosis... I begin by taking in a full, deep and satisfying breath... allowing my lungs to expand fully... holding the breath for a moment... hearing my inner signal to let go as I exhale..."

"Feeling the wonderful sensations of relaxation beginning to spread through my body... noticing how good that feels... taking three or four more deep breaths... and letting go with each exhale... (wait 60 seconds)... then, allowing my breathing to return to normal... easy... natural... effortless... breathing rhythmically... noticing how I feel... how my neck and shoulders are letting go of any tension I don't need..."

"Allowing my eyes to close... noticing how my view of everything changes... from the world outside... to the world inside... seeing images that flow across the screen in my mind... pictures that my mind creates... and bringing to mind the image of a staircase with twenty steps... visualizing the staircase in any way I wish... seeing all of it... or part of it... knowing that however I see the staircase is fine... noticing what it looks like and what it's made of... the materials, colors, textures... the handrail... wood, metal, granite... carpeting on the steps..."

"And me standing at the top ... knowing that as I count each step and go down I will become more relaxed with each step I take... one step for each number I count... I can see myself, feel myself standing at the top step... my hand on the railing... feeling its smoothness... ready to take the first step... to begin counting myself down the twenty steps... just noticing how my relaxation and comfort deepen with each step I take..."

"Now I take the first step... saying one in my mind as I exhale... two... feeling my body moving down each step... my foot sinking into the deep carpeting... this is fun... this is fine... three... noticing how much more relaxed I feel already... places in my body feeling more relaxed than other places... my neck and shoulders letting go... wondering which muscles will become more relaxed next... breathing naturally..".

"Four... settling deeper into the chair... deeper into comfort... calmer... five... restful relaxation spreading down my arms... wondering if the right arm is more relaxed than the left... or if the left feels heavier than the right... six... seeing and feeling myself take each step down the staircase... enjoying this relaxation... nothing to bother me... nothing to disturb my attention... focusing on the feelings... seven... noticing how deep the color of the carpet is... deeper in color as I go down... comfort and relaxation flowing across my scalp... down my face..."

"Nothing to disturb me... any sounds, sensations... everything a part of my experience of comfort and enjoyment... as I move down the stairs and deeper into auto-hypnosis... eight... more and more feelings of restful heaviness flowing down my arms, hands... into my chest, stomach... nine... comfortable relaxation spreading throughout my body... comfortable and in control... as I move farther down the staircase..."

"Ten... half-way down the staircase... farther down the stairs... deeper and deeper... noticing the feelings of increased heaviness... or is it lightness... eleven... deeper and deeper relaxed... nothing to bother or disturb me... the color of the carpet on the stairs becoming even more deep... deeper and more profound... twelve... thirteen... feeling, enjoying this deep relaxation... a sense of growing comfort... fourteen... relaxed... comfortable... absolutely nothing to do but enjoy these feelings..."

"Fifteen... deeper and deeper relaxed... going deeper down the stairs and experiencing increased comfort... restful... relaxed... sixteen... deeper and more comfortable... deeper than I've ever been before... and I can go even deeper... seventeen... all my focus on these pleasant and enjoyable feelings... of comfort... relaxation... trance... eighteen... knowing this experience is mine to enjoy... to appreciate... auto-hypnotically relaxed... all parts of my body relaxed and at ease... letting go of everything I don't need... nineteen... almost at the bottom of the staircase... feeling more and more relaxed... rested... comfortable... nothing to bother or disturb me... nothing to do but enjoy these sensations... this comfort..."

"And now... twenty... bottom of the staircase... feeling so deeply, deeply relaxed... deeper with every breath I take... with every moment that passes... more deeply relaxed and comfortable than I can remember... so comfortable that I want to remain in this deeply relaxed state... this state of auto-hypnosis... focusing only on my feelings... sensations... experiences... enjoying the images that flow through my mind...

"In this comfortable meditative state... feeling so safe and secure... with nothing to disturb me... nothing to bother me... no one to interfere... my thinking can be clear... my focus can be complete... in this state of deep hypnosis... I can look at issues, problems... see them more clearly... dare to explore feelings... thoughts... know that in this safe place I am free... in control... that I have access to all parts of me..."

"My unconscious mind... protecting me in so many ways... protecting my unknown potentials and abilities... it all belongs to me... and I can share it in any way I choose... with myself... because I am a unique individual... no one else quite like me... anywhere... realizing that nobody really knows their capacities... and mine are there for me to discover... in whatever way I wish... as slowly or as quickly as I would like..."

"Knowing one thing very clearly... in this wonderful, peaceful state... I can allow myself to discover many things I can do... and there are so many more than I ever dreamed there could be...because I have abilities I don't yet know about... I know I will change... but I don't know how my behavior will show it... just yet..."

"Time to awaken... to come back to conscious awareness... easy to do... no effort at all... and I can awaken as a person... while these comfortable feelings stay in my body... I may forget many things... but I can remember something important... I can return again to this comfortable state of mind... any time I wish..."

"And now I can go back to the staircase... begin to go up... one step at a time... from twenty back to one... toward being alert and aware... and as I go up each step I can find myself beginning to awaken... easily... knowing that when I reach the third step my eyes will open... and when I reach the top step I'll feel refreshed and alert... mind fully aware... keeping the feelings of being comfortable and at ease... refreshed... alert... completely and fully awake... with feelings of confidence and comfort!" (End of Script)

Practice entering into a deeply relaxed state by following one of the above scripts until you can quickly and easily slip into hypnosis. You might also use visualizations from the previous chapter that appeal to you. Record them onto audio tape and practice with them to give yourself more experience in the process and sensations of auto- hypnosis. Like any tool, deep hypnosis becomes increasingly effective as you become more familiar and comfortable using it

SELF INDUCED, AUTO-HYPNOSIS

Self-induced, auto-hypnosis is the ability to put yourself into a deep meditative state at any time you choose. It is the process of making and following suggestions you give to yourself. It is much easier to learn self-induced, auto-hypnosis when you have already had a number of experiences entering into a meditative state and know what this experience is like.

Self-induced, auto-hypnosis clearly differs from hypnosis done while listening to someone verbalizing the directions. Even though learning hypnosis is easiest when done with another person or using an audio tape, your goal is to develop the ability to enter a meditative state without having to use a tape and to do so quickly, easily and comfortably.

Auto-Hypnosis

It gives me a wonderful sense of personal power and more self-confidence.

There are a few simple yet important steps to keep in mind:

First, you are in complete control. There is no such thing as entering into a hypnotic trance and not being able to come out of it. You can arouse yourself at any time; you only have to make the decision. If you use auto-hypnosis when you're tired, the worst that can happen is your trance would simply merge into relaxed sleep.

There may be times when that is exactly what you want to do. Put yourself into a relaxed trance and give yourself suggestions for deepening relaxation until you fall asleep. Visualizing calm and soothing images can be as effective as a prescribed tranquilizer. It is certainly healthier for you.

Second, the process is safe. Auto-hypnosis is time limited. It is much like the breathing, relaxation, or visualizing exercises you have already done. Hypnosis has three distinct stages:

❶ A rather formalized beginning or induction,

❷ A middle portion when you give yourself suggestions for creativity, problem solving, or simply deep relaxation,

❸ A clearly defined ending.

You decide when to enter into trance, the depth or level you wish to reach, and the length of time you will stay hypnotized. Once you've reached the level of relaxation and hypnosis you desire, the images you'll see or problems you'll work on, and the post-meditative suggestions you make to yourself before coming back to a normal waking state are entirely up to you.

Third, suggestions made while in an hypnotic trance can be a very powerful tool for changing attitudes and behaviors. It's easy to get locked into patterns of beliefs and behaviors that may have been useful in the past but no longer work for you today. In many ways, that's what test anxiety is all about.

Test anxious students have learned to cope to deal with their pressures and fears. Unfortunately, too often the way they cope is self-defeating, and leads to poor concentration, ineffective study habits, low grades, and a negative self-image. Bad coping habits become the problem, and they're hard to change even when you are fully conscious of them.

With auto-hypnosis, your conscious mind gets to take a brief vacation as you access your unconscious mind. The unconscious has virtually no bad habits or restrictions. Time and the clock are much less important. Your unconscious mind can try anything it wishes because it doesn't worry about being exposed or embarrassed. Also, communicating with your unconscious is a very private act; no one will ever know of your internal conversations.

Self-Induced Hypnosis Script

An effective method for learning self-induced, auto-hypnosis involves pairing suggestions you make to yourself with a physical cue. The cue acts as a signal to your mind and body that you are ready to enter into a meditative state and that something out of the ordinary is about to occur. Using a cue makes it easier for you to get into a meditative frame of mind. The cue clearly establishes a boundary between relaxation and auto-hypnosis. The cue also marks the start of the self-induced, auto-hypnosis procedure. In the following script, notice the introduction of the cue during the beginning phase of your hypnosis.

"Now, I am going to allow myself... to begin to let go... to become fully relaxed... as I begin my basic auto-hypnosis routine... I am learning to drift into a meditative way of being... in a different way... all by myself... I can learn to drift into deep hypnosis for a brief time... or a longer time..."

"I determine the length of time... as I can determine when... and where... it will be useful for me to enter a meditative state... so that I can utilize my unconscious mind... to do so many things... for myself... and if I haven't already done so... I can allow my eyes to close now... to change my view of reality... from outside... to inside... from the world around me... to the world within me...

"I am about to take in a deep breath of air... and as I do so... I will make a fist... with my right hand... or my left hand... which ever feels most natural... I'll make a tight fist as I take in a deep breath of air... and notice the feelings... the tightness in the fingers... and the hand... up into the wrist and forearm... perhaps to the elbow... and then, as I begin to exhale... sending the air from my lungs... and at the same time telling myself in my mind to let go... I can relax that hand... really relax it... allowing the hand to become totally limp and loose... to become very relaxed..."

"Any tension flowing away... more and more fully at ease... feeling warmth flowing into the hand and fingers... a warm comfort that begins to spread... from the hand and up through the arm... past the elbow... into the upper arm... the shoulder... the upper part of my back and across... and down into the other arm... and when I've exhaled completely, I do it again... inhaling fully... as the same hand forms a tight fist... and hearing my thought to let go... as I exhale the air from my lungs... the hand becoming fully relaxed... loose and limp... warm... comfortable... breathing easily... naturally... without effort..."

"That relaxation continues to spread... and to increase... as it flows through my abdomen... and my neck... up across the scalp... my face... eyes relaxing deep in their sockets... as I continue to drift down... relaxed... more and more completely... feeling so good... as my legs and thighs relax... my feet... relaxing everywhere... every part of my body... all muscles letting go... the relaxation continuing to increase... as I drift down... into a wonderful trance state of mind... a hypnotic state of being..."

"My mind is relaxing as well... letting go... and it becomes easier and easier... to allow awareness... to be guided by the unconscious mind... letting the unconscious... be more and more in charge... more and more responsible... for guiding me... showing me the way... and directing my awareness... of all those experiences that can be useful to me... in so many ways..."

"And it really doesn't matter what my conscious mind does... my unconscious mind will automatically do... what it needs to do to help me... to achieve what I want for myself... as I continue to drift downward... no effort at all... nothing to bother me... or disturb me... drifting down... and up if I wish..."

"I can imagine myself... drifting slowly back up... toward the level of awareness... to give myself the opportunity... to practice once again... this new ability... this experience of putting myself... into deep hypnosis... and I can ask myself... How much of a hypnotic state... do I feel I am in already?..."

"And I inhale deeply as I make that tight fist... noticing again the tightness in the muscles... and telling myself to let go as I exhale... the hand relaxing... feeling the warmth and relaxation spreading... flowing... and I drift down again... allowing myself to go even deeper... deeper into trance... enjoying these feelings... of comfort... effortless comfort and relaxation... drifting... in my own way... taking as much time as I wish... drifting deeper and even more comfortably... and then rising again... into a lighter state of hypnosis..."

"Approaching again that surface of awareness and alertness... and giving myself permission to experience the cue... with a deep intake of air... with a tight fist... and letting go with the air that flows outward... and every muscle lets go... as I continue to learn and enjoy... this ability to take myself into hypnosis... drifting deeply yet... deeper than I've gone before... and I know now... to make that fist... how to relax the hand... and the body... to allow that comforting relaxation to spread... as I drift down... down with the relaxation... into my own state of hypnosis... in my own way... my own time... to a level I choose..."

" Easily and effortlessly... nothing to do... but to enjoy the sensations... and the feelings... with nothing to bother... nothing to disturb... simply letting go... more and more completely... and drifting down and up... and letting my unconscious mind choose the way... because it knows... what is the right way for me..."

"Now that I have learned... now that I know... and have experienced in my mind and body... this ability to drift down... in this special, effortless way... my unconscious mind is more open to me... more available for me... to hear and receive... the suggestions I give to myself... suggestions that will allow... my unconscious mind to help me... to discover what my unconscious mind can do... to achieve those things I want for myself... become comfortably relaxed... calm and at ease..."

"Able to concentrate in a peaceful and focused manner... to

study more effectively... approach tests more confidently... feeling more alive... energetic and aware... feeling good about my abilities... about myself... and I can utilize this ability... breathing deeply and making a tight fist... exhaling completely as I let go... and drifting down... more and more easily... more and more deeply... each time I do so... I can do this anytime... and anywhere I wish... in my own time... in my own way... giving my unconscious mind an opportunity... to help me take care of these things that are important to me...and all I have to do is drift down... and drift back up..."

"Drifting back upwards... now... in my own fashion... taking all the time I need... drifting back towards the surface of alertness... bringing everything I've learned with me... becoming more and more aware... and as I drift upwards... my unconscious mind knows... it can return to this relaxed and comfortable state... can return easily and naturally... to work constructively for me... and now, back to awareness... feeling refreshed and alert... and a comfortable self-awareness... and as I reach full awareness... full alertness... I can allow my eyes to open... feeling renewed, refreshed and wide, wide awake!" (End of Script)

This basic self-induced, auto-hypnosis script gives you complete discretion regarding how long you choose to experience a trance and how deep you wish to go. The depth of trance will vary. Each practice session strengthens the mind-body response and puts you more in control. It's easy to apply the tight-fist-deep-breathing technique to a wide variety of uses such as triggering a relaxation response or focusing your thinking on a problem or task.

SUMMING UP

Using your innate talents to achieve an altered state of consciousness, you've learned how to change negative self-images into positive affirmations. You'll explore this topic in greater depth in Step 5: Seeing The World A Different Way.

Step 5: SEEING THE WORLD A DIFFERENT WAY

Changing beliefs from negative to positive

*"Believe that life is worth living,
and your belief will create the fact."*

William James

This comment by William James sums up the theme of Step 5. Test anxious students often believe they cannot, and will not, do well. They develop a negative internal dialogue. They anticipate failure and no longer expect success. They minimize, overlook, or drown their personal abilities, strengths, and assets in a sea of pessimistic beliefs.

This chapter illustrates the differences between positive and negative thinking. It shows you what to do about changing your internal dialogue from expected failure to anticipated success.

SELF-DEFEATING THINKING

"I really can't do it, anyway." "I'm going to blow it no matter how hard I try." "Taking tests is horrible; I always fail." These comments by test-anxious individuals reflect a set of beliefs that fit what sociologist Robert Merton describes as a self-fulfilling prophecy. Merton explains this as the prediction an individual makes to her or himself about something that will occur. The person then acts in a way to make the prediction come true.

"I really can't do it" is another way of saying, "I don't believe I can succeed, so I'll only confirm my belief when I do badly."

Negative thinking is the internal expression of worry. It's very difficult to expect to succeed or to do well when you hear a voice in your head telling you you're going to do lousy. The reasons are quite clear. Worried or negative thinking does nothing good for test performance.

Negative messages quickly become self-reinforcing. They're difficult to refute or put aside. Your mind focuses on these extraneous thoughts that have nothing to do with the test questions. So much effort goes into negative and irrelevant thinking you can't focus clearly or remember important facts and information. You believe, quite correctly, that you knew the material before the test began. It's no wonder so many test-anxious students say they "blank out" when they take a test.

Thinking and Test Anxiety

Psychiatrist Aaron Beck says that your conscious thoughts play a primary role in how you experience emotions and behave in your everyday life. He believes that on-going anxiety and depression result from automatic self-negating and self-defeating thinking or visualizing. Beck characterized negative thoughts or images as too absolute, too broad or extreme, or too arbitrary.

Beck noted three themes that illustrate distorted thinking, and noted how they are associated with a self-defeating outlook. They are:

❶ When you interpret events negatively.

❷ When you dislike yourself.

❸ When you view the future negatively.

In effect, you bad-mouth yourself and tend to personalize your failures. You may find yourself interpreting even minor errors as major goofs. That leads you to over-generalize your faults, and decide after one mistake that nothing else you do will turn out right. By then it's easy to get lost in the details and lose sight of your overall task or goal.

If this description fits, you have basic negative assumptions that form the core of your beliefs. It is those beliefs that influence the way you deal with life. Studying, getting ready for, or taking tests with a self-defeating outlook makes taking a test very difficult.

It is as though you were starting a hike or a climb toting a heavy knapsack. Instead of carrying food and other things that are good for you, your knapsack is filled with large rocks. The stones are your negative beliefs and they're weighing you down. Very simply, your beliefs are keeping you from climbing the hill to good grades.

Musterbating and Awfulizing

Albert Ellis said that psychological disorders and poor personal performance "... arise from faulty or irrational patterns of thinking. The thought patterns typically express themselves in chains of preconscious, implicit verbalizations." According to Ellis, these are the core assumptions that make up the person's basic belief system. Ellis states that irrational thoughts are self-defeating or have self-destructive consequences.

"I have got to do well!" "I must get a high score." "It will be awful if I do badly." Ellis describes such statements as "musturbating" and "awfulizing." He describes how such thoughts are the basis for internal responses that give rise to negative emotions. The student interprets the self-messages as an increased pressure to do well.

Each *must, should, have to, can't,* or whatever, is a demand for perfection that becomes increasingly difficult to meet.

Excess worry about failing increases the likelihood of failure. Like a wheel, negative, self-defeatist thinking rolls along, reinforcing itself with each cycle of pressure, doubt, and lack of success. The student becomes pessimistic about being able to succeed at all.

Both Ellis and Merton wrote that individuals who expect to do badly have beliefs that lead to a pattern of failure. These students often find it difficult to commit enough time and energy to succeed. Their energies get turned inward toward themselves, instead of outward toward the tasks to be accomplished. They also procrastinate, and avoid working on anything related to school. As a result, they do badly on tests. Unless negative thinking changes, students can remain stuck in a self-defeating cycle that may go on for years.

Making a Change

Sandra felt mentally "weak" when it came to numbers. She didn't know how the image was formed or when it began. She was simply aware that as far back as she could remember, everyone expected her to do badly at arithmetic. As she progressed through school her grades were generally good in most subjects, but never in math. No matter how prepared she felt, "something" would sabotage her efforts each time she took a math test. She either made careless mistakes, "forgot" what she really knew, or ran out of time.

Every failure only confirmed her sense that she was inadequate. The feelings spread like a sneaky weed to other areas. She accepted that she was not "supposed" to do well. Before she could do well in math and get good grades on tests, she had to change her beliefs.

With time and effort she found she really could do fine in math. Sandra's overall outlook began to improve and become more positive. A new, more positive self-image gradually replaced the old, negative one. A more positive belief-system developed, one that expects success instead of failure.

Improve self-confidence from that to THIS!

OPTIMISM VERSUS PESSIMISM

Expecting success is the opposite of anticipating failure. When you succeed at test taking, or any endeavor, you have a positive self-image. Your self-confidence increases. You become more optimistic about the future. You believe that with the right effort, you deserve success and you'll attain it. Obviously, committing to a goal is much easier when you're optimistic about accomplishing it from the start.

Psychologist Martin Seligman discovered a major difference between optimists and pessimists. Optimistic individuals tend to attribute failure to something they did wrong. Pessimists attribute failure to something wrong with themselves.

Optimists know they can alter or resolve the problem. They don't believe failures are the result of a built-in weakness they can't change. Confidence in their power to effect change, both within themselves and in the things they do, is self-reinforcing.

Pessimists fear they can't solve anything. Since the problem is in them, they don't feel they have the power to make meaningful changes. Pessimistic, defeatist beliefs are also self-reinforcing, in an opposite and much less desirable way.

Optimism and a positive attitude go hand-in-hand. You feel confident that you can deal with the occasional failure or setback. As Seligman points out, everyone stumbles occasionally. Students with strong self-esteem can see a poor performance in the proper perspective. They don't take a bad test score as a sign of personal inadequacy. Rather, they see failures as learning experiences and lessons for improving future performances.

Putting Yourself In Control

A positive self-image puts you more in control. You know what to expect and how to best prepare for tests. You'll see and approach the world as it is, not as a fantasy and not as you might *wish* it to be. Author William Saroyan said, "Dreams are what make life worth living." That means you can have dreams, but you don't attempt to live life in a dream.

When you're optimistic, you can put a positive spin on even tough situations. You want to succeed, not just for the grades but also to avoid feeling bad when you fail. In the same way that negative thinking is like a deflated ball that loses speed as it rolls, positive thinking can also be seen as a ball, but one that is rolling easily and smoothly down a hill. As it rolls along, the ball's speed increases.

Your confidence gets a forward thrust when you support and reinforce it with positive thoughts and images. You feel motivated and better about yourself.

Changing Negative Thinking

"I can't do this." "What will my parents think of me if I don't do well on this test?" "I wonder how everybody else is doing and how much farther ahead of me they are?" "How did the smart students answer this question?" "What if I flunk the exam?"

These are anxiety provoking, negative thoughts. Just keep these thoughts in your head if you want to feel bad about yourself, think you can't do much, and have a poor self-image. All of them are downers. None of them is directed toward finding a solution to a problem or coming up with an answer to a test question.

Negative thinking is very distracting. It reduces your focus and concentration on the test material and makes it tougher for you to correctly answer the questions.

Try the following statements and see how comfortable you are with them: "What information do I need to answer this question?" "I can remember this diagram from the reading and the class notes." "I am doing the best I can and my efforts feel good." "I am going to remain calm and keep my cool. I can always keep my cool!" Positive statements focus on the task. You'll always do better when your focus, effort, and concentration are on the test contents, and worse when your mental efforts are on something else.

You can't do well when you're preoccupied with worried thinking, over-anxious feelings, or comparing yourself with how the other students are doing. There's always some straight "A" student who may do better than you. Worrying about it won't help you get a higher score. You need to chill out and *think* about your *thinking*.

Checking Your Thoughts

According to Beck's and Ellis' theories, the first step in changing negative thinking is:

❶ Become aware of the stream of thoughts and self-verbalizations that continually pass through your mind.

❷ Determine the impact negative thinking has on what you're doing, in school and elsewhere.

❸ Question whether the thoughts are valid. Look at your negative thinking in the light of reality. Irrational thoughts are either truly false, or else constructed so that they can't be verified.

To repeat, self-defeating thoughts lead to negative emotions. You end up asking yourself to prove that YOU are thoroughly competent and successful at all times. You *must* accomplish (something...anything) to be acceptable to people who are important to you. These thoughts are not rational and they can't be proven.

Dealing With Irrational Thinking

Beck and Ellis would encourage you to confront your irrational thinking as a first step toward changing it. Consider the following self-defeating statement: "I cannot disappoint my parents or they'll think I'm worthless."

❶ Restate the thought and look at its individual parts. "I cannot disappoint my parents" is the first part and, "or they'll think I'm worthless." is the remainder. Realistically, you may need high grades on a particular test in order to qualify for the college of your choice, enter graduate school, pass the bar, or whatever. But, the second statement does not automatically follow from the first, and certainly is not necessarily true.

❷ Change your negative thinking to get a more realistic view of the situation. You'll improve your state of mind and your self-image. Presumably, you don't want to fail. In all likelihood, the people who care about you don't want to see you fail either. Chances are, you'll strive to do the best you can. Certainly, you will be disappointed because you did not achieve a desired grade, but that doesn't mean you are worthless and unacceptable.

❸ It is important to differentiate between what is true and real versus what is clearly irrational. Negative thoughts are generally quite narrow in scope and limit your range of personal outcomes at school and in life. Success becomes the only allowable measure. If you fail the test you're inept. If you don't do well you are stupid.

❹ Absolute statements leave little room for alternatives. *Musts, shoulds,* and *have tos* are all ultimatums and demands for perfection. They place a tremendous, self-imposed burden on YOU.

The truth is, it's okay to not have to get an "A" every time you take an exam. Earning a 4.0 grade point average and making the dean's list or Phi Beta Kappa is a goal, not a mandate. Success is not measured in absolutes. Life would be boring if it consisted only of blacks and whites and contained no range of colors and gray.

❺ Lastly, no test outcome is a measure of your self-worth. You may do great on a test today, and blow one tomorrow. Neither an A or an F is a reflection of your true value as a person. Think about it. If only one test score determined a person's worth, we would all be in very deep trouble.

Confront, Confront, Confront

Evaluating a situation realistically forms the basis for more positive thought patterns. Vigorously confronting negative thinking or self-imaging whenever it occurs is equally important. Become aware of negative thoughts going through your mind. Then loudly and firmly give yourself positive statements to counter them. Do it often. Slipping back into defeatist thinking is extremely easy.

When you experience positive thoughts and images you take a major step toward feeling better about yourself. Think success, and you're more likely to expect success. This is especially true when you couple your expectations with accomplishment.

YOU <u>ARE</u> NUMBER ONE

Having self-affirming thoughts and verbalization is like a mental and emotional rehearsal for how you'll perform in the future. When you have a mental picture of yourself doing well, it becomes easier to believe you will succeed. Each small improvement is a good reason to anticipate more improvement.

When you believe success is coming, your positive thoughts encourage greater possibilities for successful studying and test-taking. They create a wider range of choices about how you can feel and act. Assertive and self-empowering statements define your goals and focus your energies. They should emphasize what you *want* to do, not what you *must* or *need* to do.

Vary Your Affirmations

Don't stick with just one affirmative statement. Remember when you were a child and played the game of saying your own name over and over again? Soon your name began to sound like gibberish and it quickly made no sense at all. The same thing can happen with affirmations. A single affirmative statement used over and over will quickly lose its meaning and impact.

Compose a number of positive statements that feel inspiring when played in your head. "I know the material and I am prepared." "I am going to do well on this and my other exams." "I will do the very best I am capable of and I will feel proud of my efforts." "Even if I blow this exam, it does not mean I am stupid and worthless." Develop the habit of practicing positive self-statements at all times, not just when studying or preparing to take a test.

THINKING AND MOTIVATION

Your attitude strongly influences how well or how poor you will do in a class. This is especially true when the course you are taking isn't very exciting or perhaps is a subject in which you have little interest. It's hard to get motivated when you don't like what you're doing. The more focus you place on how miserable you are, the harder it will be for you to accomplish anything. Concentrating on the negative begins that downward spiral of procrastination, poor study and grades, and a loss of self-esteem.

Find the Good Stuff

You don't take a class without a good reason. It may be a course required for graduation or classes needed to achieve specific academic or career goals. Whatever the purpose for being in that classroom, you owe it to yourself to give any course your best effort. There is something in the subject that can stimulate your interest and curiosity if you are open to seeing it.

Carol described science classes as uninteresting, and the instructor as stuffy and boring. She found herself fighting to stay awake in class. She quickly became more frustrated with the subject and with school.

She received an invitation to visit her grandparents and stay with them during a school break. Carol didn't usually enjoy going to their house because, as she said, "There wasn't much to do." She went because it was an opportunity to escape her regular routine for a short period.

Her grandparents' home was located in the country, on the edge of a forested area that sloped down to the ocean. It was a perfect place for walking, which Carol didn't especially enjoy. On previous visits she had gone to the nearby woods or shore-line only when her grandfather asked for her company.

After a day of lying around the house Carol found herself restless and bored. Almost in desperation she decided to stroll one of the many paths. Leaving the house, she wandered down to the rocky shore-line at the base of a wooded hill and soon found herself jumping from stone to stone. For the first time Carol noticed the small sea urchins and other creatures that lived in the watery hollows and buried themselves in amongst the rocks. Her interest was aroused as she watched them, and she marveled at the way they scrambled about from one place to another.

On a later walk among the trees she saw a doe and two young fawns. She watched as they browsed and marveled at how the fawns' spotted coats allowed them to become almost invisible among the trees. They seemed to disappear as they moved through the light and shadow. Each day Carol found more hidden nooks, holes, trees and areas to explore. For the first time, a visit to her grandparents home ended too soon.

When she returned to school, the instructor was just as stuffy but Carol's interest in the subject was now aroused. She decided to get what she could from her classes, solely for her own enjoyment and benefit. Without any apparent additional effort, her grades headed "up" along with her attitude about school.

THE PLEASURES OF REWARDING YOURSELF

Every success deserves a reward. Perhaps you remember when you were young and did your household chores extra well. Chances are you received a reward. Perhaps it was a trip to the ice cream store or even the toy store. That unexpected treat probably made the chores more endurable and even a lot more fun.

Studies confirm that rewarding yourself for attaining a goal reinforces your gains and helps you look forward to the next challenge. The size of the accomplishment doesn't seem to matter. Very simply, rewards are strong incentives to succeed.

Don't reward yourself only when you ace an exam. An old Chinese proverb says, "The journey of a thousand miles begins with the first step." You deserve a reward after each step as you learn to relax better, develop your visualizing skills, improve study habits, and do any of the other exercises in this book.

Positive Reinforcement

Always reward yourself immediately after you have successfully done the job you set out to do. If you wait too long or make the reward too hard to achieve, it will not mean as much and you may feel it is not worth the effort it takes to get it. If that is the case, your self-reward could end up feeling more like self-punishment.

Your self-reward can be small, but it should be one you look forward to and will enjoy. Rachel described how she planned her study schedule to include time for quick jogs around the block. She loved running and chose little bursts of jogging as her reward for completing each period of studying. As an added value, Rachel found the physical activity helped relieve any muscle tension that built up as she concentrated on her books and notes.

Jonathan made going to a movie his self-reward after completing a term paper. He had always been a procrastinator, but for this assignment he changed his usual study pattern by planning a schedule and sticking to it rather than waiting until the last minute. After finishing the paper, Jonathan came to the conclusion that no matter what the grade received, he had done his best. He felt good about his efforts and rewarded himself for his hard work and dedication. Most of all, his reward was for approaching and completing the task in a different way.

Making Rewards Work

Self-rewards can take the form of favorite activities, special treats, or tokens of some kind. You can accumulate a number of small rewards in exchange for a "big" prize after you complete the project. For the student whose reward was going to a movie, he might have given himself some small amount toward the total cost of the movie after completing each study or writing session. The size and kind of reward should fit your needs and be in line with the effort you make.

In each case there are additional rewards that accompany well-earned higher grades. These are the internal rewards of knowing you did a job well, and the expectation you'll get the same good results next time. Internal rewards reinforce your desire to see your behavior in a positive and affirming way. They encourage you to see yourself in a positive light. Success breeds success, which leads to a positive self-image, and that is the essence of self-confidence.

SUMMING UP

The differences between positive and negative thinking can be the difference between success and failure in school and beyond. Changing your internal dialogue from negative to positive statements frees you from disabling worry and anxiety.

Chapter 6: Improving The Odds, introduces techniques for studying and test-taking that build on your expectations of success and increase your skills and self-confidence.

Step 6: IMPROVING THE ODDS

New Ways to Study, Learn, and Remember

"You cannot create experience, you must undergo it."

Albert Camus

STUDY SMARTS

Good study habits are vital. You could be the most relaxed test taker in the world, but if you don't know the material, you'll simply be the most relaxed failure. By itself, relaxation won't do a thing to improve your grades.

As you experience many of the techniques described in this chapter, you will discover new and effective strategies for improving your study skills. You'll learn methods used by many students to develop new thinking strategies.

There are any number of paths to the top of a mountain, and there are many routes you can take that lead to improved study and test-taking skills. All the various methods that follow work in concert with the relaxation and imaging techniques you have already learned. Each of the methods is an assist for you to reach your goals of higher scores and reduced anxiety.

Being Prepared

If you were going to climb a high mountain, you wouldn't wait for the day of the trek to plan your ascent. Careful preparation would include finding out as much as you could about the weather, what clothing to take, the best equipment to use and so on. You would study the maps and plan your route well in advance. In short, you'd prepare for your climb long before the departure date to insure an exciting, safe, and enjoyable adventure.

Climbers who don't plan ahead risk failure or worse. They're like many test-anxious students who also don't plan ahead very well. They usually have poor study skills and use time very inefficiently. Many prepare for tests by spending countless hours with their noses buried in their books and papers. Unfortunately, what they read doesn't seem to stick around for long.

Others avoid feeling anxious about an upcoming test by doing everything except studying until the last minute. Then they spend whatever time remains cramming until the wee hours. Clearly, the majority of students with test-anxiety don't prepare for tests in easy stages; they struggle through a continual last stage.

Study Well, Not Long

Research shows, it isn't how much time you study that counts — it's how efficiently you study. The quantity of time is not nearly so important as how well you use the time.

Studying effectively instead of cramming at the last minute doesn't increase your anxiety. On the contrary, a good study program reduces anxious feelings and has the added bonus of taking less time and energy.

Step 1 in developing study smarts is getting an early start. Think about preparing for a test before the class has even met for the first time. You'll find here are many advantages. For instance, it's very helpful to have some idea of what the course is about before attending the first class. You're mentally preparing for the material that's coming. New information and new terms won't overwhelm you. You'll be in a position to approach the topics and ideas in your own way and at your own speed.

Starting early gives you an idea of the course goals. Most important, you have the advantage of preparing for exams from the get-go.

Step 2 is reading in the most effective manner, and that means being able to retain material for longer than thirty seconds. In a few short minutes, the average person loses approximately half the new information and ideas he or she has just read.

New knowledge first goes into short-term memory. After being reinforced through additional reading and studying, the material progresses into long-term memory. In this way the information becomes "learned," and will stick around for the long haul.

Step 3 involves preparing for class by briefly previewing the material to be presented. With a basic understanding new information doesn't sound totally foreign. You'll learn more completely and it'll be easier to take notes. Clearly, you can't to do this step if the information isn't in class handouts or in your text.

Step 4 is learning to take effective notes. Good notes are the single most effective way to review new knowledge and commit it to memory. Once memorized, the material is readily available for quick recall. Taking good notes is an elementary skill. It makes all the other study and test-taking techniques described in this book work better for you.

SMART READING

You have to read new information to learn it. However, simply reading a selection of text does not guarantee you'll understand or retain it. That's because reading to learn is very different from reading for enjoyment. Unlike a good novel, when you read to learn and understand, the least efficient method is to start at the first page in a chapter and read straight through to the last page.

First, begin your reading by skimming the chapter or section. Numerous studies demonstrate that skimming is an efficient way to remember new information. Carefully read the titles and everything that catches your eye or stands out from the ordinary text.

Second, browse the rest, and pay particular attention to the summarizing paragraphs. This will give you a fast review of the material as well as a quick sense of the ideas being presented.

Third, quickly read the entire chapter or selection. Make mental notes of the important or significant parts. Put a check mark by the ideas you don't understand. When you've finished, go back and reread the checked paragraphs more slowly until you fully understand the material.

Fourth, if the ideas still don't make sense even after you've gone over it one or two more times, *get help*. See your instructor, find a tutor, or talk with fellow students who seem to have grasped the concepts. Do not simply reread the passage over and over, hoping it will eventually sink into your brain. Reading a passage again and again is frustrating, fatiguing, and a waste of time and energy.

Writing for Recall

After you've read the material, write a brief summary in your own words. I suggest you use one of the note taking techniques described below. Good notes help fix new ideas and information more firmly in your mind. Use a few key words or sentences to identify any significant details or major points.

Writing strengthens learning and memory in a number of ways. The physical work of putting words on paper enhances memory by involving the muscles of your body as well as the muscle of your mind. Writing takes concentration. Making the effort and thinking about an idea helps you learn it. Writing also acts as a filter by eliminating unnecessary material and narrowing your focus to the important items and ideas.

To Highlight or Not to Highlight

Stifle the urge to highlight everything that "seems" important. What you'll end up with is a book full of highlighted pages. The parts you don't highlight are the one that will stand out. Underlining or highlighting too many words or passages kills the entire reason of marking them for quick identification. Highlighting is only effective when used sparingly. Highlighted passages enable you to quickly pick out major points or ideas from the rest of the words on the page.

Another waste of effort is underlining or highlighting a passage before first skimming the entire selection. How will you know what major facts or ideas to look for?

It Pays to Go to Class

It especially pays to be particularly attentive during the first and last few minutes of a class lecture. The first five minutes is often when material that will be covered during the class is previewed or outlined by the instructor.

The last five minutes is usually the most valuable class time of all. It is the period most instructors use to sum up the lecture and to emphasize the vital points most likely to be on a test. It is also the time when you can catch up on any notes you may have missed writing during the lecture.

Style Isn't Everything, But...

While in class, pay careful attention to your instructor's speech and style of lecturing. Notice the overall approach. If the instructor follows the textbook, you can outline your notes before class and fill them in as the lecture progresses. When an instructor normally addresses only important or difficult issues, you need to cover the chapter quite thoroughly before attending class.

Instructors often add information not found in the class text. Plan to write more complete notes that include the additional material. Be alert when the instructor emphasizes or favors certain words and phrases. Write these down verbatim! They will probably be included in the next exam.

Identify and focus on the essential information being presented. This includes key ideas and principles, theories, and all the material relating to the primary focus of the course. Note particularly the topics or areas where the instructor spends the most time. You can just about bet the farm that you'll encounter this material on a test. Examples can include slides the instructor shows in class or what you find written on the board. Clearly, if the material wasn't important the instructor would not spend the time and effort putting it on the board or presenting it to you.

GENERAL NOTE TAKING STRATEGIES

One of the best ways to enhance learning and get a higher grade is by taking organized and succinct notes. Good notes usually include about a quarter of what the instructor says, word-for-word. The remaining notes should focus on material you've not yet read or learned. That doesn't mean you need to write the instructor's every word down verbatim.

If the main information seems to come too fast, work to get down words that identify broad areas or topics and fill in what's missing as soon as class is over. Don't make the mistake of telling yourself you'll remember the lecture well enough to put it down later. The sooner you generate your class notes, the better your recall! New material is very fickle when not quickly reinforced. If you wait too long, the information will vanish from your short term memory like a puff of smoke in a stiff breeze.

Do's and Don'ts

Here are a few basic note-taking do's and don'ts.

First, do take notes. The simple, physical act of taking notes requires thinking about what you've heard and read. Putting words on paper automatically involves your brain and its incredible ability to analyze and organize information into some meaningful order. You're much less likely to overlook important points. Students who rely solely on their memory of a lecture too often miss the important details.

Second, *never* attempt to write down everything the instructor says. Unless you have the skills of an old-fashioned stenographer, a job almost as extinct as the dodo bird or passenger pigeon, the task is virtually impossible because the words come too fast.

More important, you'll have a difficult time with the demanding jobs of writing the instructor's every word while attempting to focus and learn new ideas. It's like trying to accomplish two very different objectives at the same time. Writing the words is one task, and understanding the ideas conveyed by the words is quite another.

Research with thousands of college and high school students strongly suggests that students who attempt to write it all down don't generally do well on exams. They find themselves too busy writing to remember what the instructor talked about. As a result, they fail to grasp the ideas being presented.

Third, it's a poor idea to tape record class lectures. You might think that a recorder would allow you to concentrate more on the material being presented. Studies show, however, that if you tape class lectures you will tend to pay less attention in class, not more. The same research indicates that average students using a tape recorder actually learn less and get lower grades. You're less likely to pay attention and listen to what's being said when the tape is running. There is also the likelihood that you won't replay the tape.

Additionally, it takes longer to transcribe a tape than to record it. Transcribing notes from a tape is a lot of bother. You'll spend much more time and effort than taking accurate lecture notes in the first place.

Organizing Your Notes

There are three basic modes of organizing notes based on the material being presented. These are:

❶   Time sequencing (chronological, used for history courses);

❷   Order sequencing (as in the periodic tables of elements, or a listing of the planets from the sun);

❸   Logical sequencing (the most complex and difficult, but the most comprehensive note-taking method)

Logical sequencing is the recommended choice for the majority of college courses. Since few lecturers present material in a logical order, it's important for you to rewrite your notes into outline form to put them into some logical arrangement.

Notes organized logically will vary in format depending on the course. You can arrange your notes from general to specific, most to least, least to most, or in whatever order works best for the subject.

Good notes done correctly are a passport to easier learning and higher grades. There are probably a dozen models for effective note taking being taught in schools today. The two techniques explained below are quite simple. Students report they work well. Plan on practicing enough for the method you choose to become comfortable and familiar. Should neither method for taking notes prove to be the right answer for you, feel free to design your own.

Key Word Technique

This is your basic, easy method for taking notes. Doing notes this way enhances learning and helps jog your memory each time you review them.

❶   Use 8 1/2 x 11 inch notebook paper. Write the main topic at the top of the page. Then, divide the page into two vertical sections as follows: draw a line that is 3-inches from the top edge, and a second that is 3 to 4-inches from the left edge. Leave room at the bottom of the page for any special notes or observations that are good memory-joggers. You'll have a page with two columns that looks like the illustration shown to the right.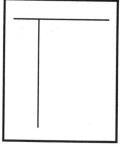

❷   The right column is for notes as you usually write them.

They should be brief, concise, and include the exact wording when the instructor is emphasizing the material.

❸ The left column is your key to effective note taking and higher grades. This is where you put the key-words that relate to the longer notes you write in the right hand column. Key-words should refer directly to the topics and any important points covered in the class lecture or the text.

❹ Use the key-word technique for taking notes from your readings as well as for class lectures. As you read, be sure not to skip over or ignore words you don't know. Write them down and look them up later. A single word can be the key to understanding an entire section of assigned text.

Using the key-word technique is very simple. As soon as possible after the lecture, review the notes you wrote in the right column. Add anything you may have omitted and make any necessary corrections. Then, in the left hand column, write key-words that relate directly to the material covered in your notes. Use your own words to identify what you'll need to pay attention to.

You're automatically thinking in a logical fashion about your notes when you choose key-words. You're considering what the words refer to and what they mean. Good key-words act to enhance recall, by solidifying both short and long term memories. Reviewing for a test becomes a snap because the memory-enhancing words you developed from your own analysis are in the key column. Remember, key-words are mind joggers, your very own personal memory enhancers.

Peruse It or Lose It

New information fades from memory very quickly. Material gets implanted more completely into your brain cells when you review it shortly after you first learn it. Enhance your memory by taking thorough notes and doing a good job of selecting logical key-words. Key-words come from your thinking about the subject.

When making notes from the reading, don't directly copy the words from the book. That is simply an exercise in penmanship. Instead, think about the material and what it means to you. Then, translate the concepts and ideas into your own words. The topics will make more sense, you'll learn the material more quickly and thoroughly. It'll be easier to remember because you've used more of your brain-power in writing the notes and then simplifying them.

Picture Technique

This is a very efficient, graphically oriented, note-taking method. It combines words and line to create a note-taking picture for better review and recall.

Picture notes work well with subjects such as biology, psychology, or the social sciences. For these subjects, picture notes divide the themes and ideas into smaller and smaller parts to make them clearly illustrated and understood.

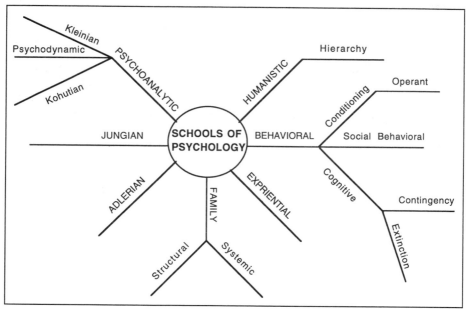

For example, psychology includes a number of major theories regarding human behavior. Each theory may have numerous conceptual approaches. Each approach includes a set of basic criteria and a particular view of diagnosis and treatment. A theory's particular approach also includes definitions, examples, sub-topics, and similar items. Picture style lecture notes describing the various schools of psychology might look like the illustration shown above.

Picture notes are easiest and work best when you do them as outlined in the following steps. While reading the instructions, you may note the similarity to a branching tree. The major exception is that the branches can go in all directions, including downward.

❶ First, draw a circle, square, or other graphic pattern in the middle of a page. In the center of the pattern print the overall title of the topic.

❷ Print the major categories or ideas on lines drawn out from the main circle.

❸ You can then draw supporting information on lines that branch from the main-ideas.

Picture-notes, or graphs, are used daily in business and industry. Their value lies in the way they illustrate and clarify information. Graphs and charts provide a quick explanation for complicated or detailed data and facts. You can clearly see the links that connect various elements, and easily add further information as needed. Well-done picture-notes can be understood at a glance, and help learning and memory in three ways:

❶ Like virtually all graphic images, they are easier to remember than words.

❷ Reviewing your notes will be quicker since a fast peek can cover a good deal of information.

❸ You won't become bored with your notes. No two lectures are identical so the picture-notes from each will be different. Plus, you won't be looking at a steady stream of wordy pages.

A Few More Note Taking Tips

The following little secrets will make note-taking easier and can pay big dividends at test-taking time.

■ Use an informal form of shorthand or speed-writing whenever possible. It doesn't have to be a recognized method. The trick is to use abbreviations without losing readability.

■ Simply eliminating vowels from words and not putting periods after abbreviations makes writing go faster. If your shorthand causes confusion, rethink what you're doing and the method you are using. Notes must be easy to read and understand to be useful.

■ Symbols can also make your shorthand more effective. Use any symbol that has meaning for you to make note-taking faster or to highlight important ideas, topics or passages. They're a shorthand for recalling complex or extensive material.

Math symbols are one example: Use the + sign for plus or

including, > for greater or more than, and its counterpart < for less than, and so on. A w/ is often used for "with." Create your own symbols and let your imagination be your guide. Just be sure you're consistent with the symbols and abbreviations you use for your personal shorthand system.

■ Rewrite and condense your notes each time you review them. This increases and improve your understanding and memory of the subject. Every rewrite invites additional thinking and analysis that leads to better memory and higher grades.

■ Never use someone else's notes. It can be a fast path to disaster for three reasons: (1) You're trusting another person's thinking and accuracy. (2) You shortchange yourself by cutting out the analyzing and organizing part of note-taking. (3) You lose the automatic part of taking notes that strengthens memory.

Remember; Writing things down, in itself, reinforces memory.

"Learning" is the act of identifying and understanding facts and ideas, while "memorizing" or "remembering" is putting those facts and ideas into mental storage for later retrieval. Memory refers to the information you've stored in various locations in your brain and the processes you use to retrieve it into consciousness. Even though you don't have to understand something to put it into memory, it should be obvious you need both learning and memory to do well in school and beyond.

In many ways, memory is like people: It comes in a multitude of different sizes and shapes. It also comes in various strengths and forms. Memory varies from the visual and auditory to the memory held in your muscles. There is short-term memory and long-term memory. Your brain's visual, auditory, and sequential systems express virtually all the various forms of memory.

Memory For Learning

The type of memory you need for improving grades is memory used to store information. This kind comes in two forms: short-term and long-term. Items placed in short-term memory stay around for limited time periods that may be very brief. Remembering a telephone number until you write it down, or a brief grocery list only until you finish shopping, are examples of items held in short-term memory.

Long-term memory stays with you for months, years, even for a lifetime. Few people who lived through it will forget where they were and what they were doing at the moment they heard of President John F. Kennedy's assassination. In a more current vein, virtually all residents of Los Angeles will forever remember the earthquake that struck in the early morning hours of January 17, 1994. Experiential, long-term memory is more permanent because it includes emotional as well as cognitive elements.

Memorizing and Recalling

As opposed to using very short-term memory, you, the student, need to remember information for at least a few days, generally from when you study the material until you finish taking the test.

Your brain has four methods it can use to accomplish the task of storing information: by pairs, categories, chains, or rules. These are the various modes any brain has for putting information into longer term memory.

Pairs memory occurs when you retain information in such a way that remembering one item brings a second item to mind. For instance, names and images go together easily. When you remember a person's name it brings a face to mind, and a mental image of the face triggers your recall of the name. You associate "Jeep," "4-wheel drive," or "off-road" with a certain type of vehicle. The name of your favorite song brings the music and lyrics to you, or hearing the words may bring the melody to mind.

Categories of information can include a multitude of items. "Vehicles" could be the heading for a major category that includes types, uses, parts, dealers, manufacturers, and much more. Categories usually have multiple sub-groupings that are then divided into progressively smaller groups of items. The first sub-group under the "vehicle" category might be manufacturers. Under the manufacturers heading you might list vehicle types, followed by the various models of this class built by the same manufacturer.

Rules are probably most students' least favorite method of memorizing material. Though they can be fun, rules lend themselves more to rote memory and less to creative visualizing. You use them most often when taking classes in the sciences, writing, or in language courses. An example might be the spelling rule of *i* before *e* except after *c* (except for the exceptions, of course). Another example is arithmetic, where 3 x 2 = 6, 3 x 3 = 9... and so on.

The more complex the rule, the more troublesome it is to memorize. Breaking the rule into smaller segments and creating an image for each part can help make remembering rules more enjoyable and a great deal easier.

For instance, the Pythagorean Theorem is expressed mathematically as $a^2 + b^2 = c^2$. Now, create a visualization to help cement the formula into your memory. Virtually everyone remembers having to learn their ABCs, and the kids who studied too hard or were "too smart" quickly got branded as nerds or squares. You might imagine each letter in a square box.

Another option is to let your imagination run a bit wilder and create a nerd-like character with a square body, scraggly hair and large feet as shown to the right. Vary the image to suit your fancy.

As with spelling and punctuation, some students learn rules quite readily while others find it rather difficult. The trick is to find the memory methods that work for you, and then to practice those methods until they're like second nature to you.

Chains are a set of connected links between items. Cursive writing is a linking of letters together to form words. When you are physically active, your muscles respond in a coordinated chain. Each muscle movement leads to the next in a smooth progression that continues until you complete the desired action. You're rarely aware of using the chaining process as you study or go through your daily activities.

Studying is a good example. It's best when you study in a coordinated series of movements and activities. At the chosen time you lay out your study material, notes and books. You settle comfortably into your chair, close your eyes and prepare yourself mentally and physically. Once relaxed and ready to learn, you pick up the papers and begin learning and memorizing the information.

PROGRAMMING YOUR STUDY PERIOD

This section deals with using a part of your personal makeup to make the job of studying a lot easier and more productive.

Cycles and Rhythms

Just about everyone is familiar with the after-lunch, early afternoon let-down, that time of the day when it's hard to concentrate and think. A short time later your energy level picks up and you become fully productive again. These periodic energy swings are more evident in some people than they are in others.

Every person has a natural, daily cycle or rhythm. You have periods of normal activity which are interspersed with shorter periods when you might experience either bouncing energy, numbing lethargy, or something in between the two.

Your overall cycle determines whether you are a night or day person. Do you bounce out of bed at the crack of dawn, alert and eager to get going, or are you the sluggish kind that has trouble getting started if the day starts too early? Are you "out of gas" by 10:00 or 10:30 p.m., or someone whose engine doesn't begin to rev until the sun goes down?

Knowing your particular biological rhythm will help determine the best times for you to study and learn. Early-in-the-day people usually do their best work in the morning hours. They accomplish more in less time and using less effort, often by studying before classes begin. Conversely, late-at-nighters should take advantage of their special internal clock by planning a study schedule for evening hours. It's quiet and their studying will rarely be interrupted.

Small swings of one, two, or three hour duration normally take place within your overall day or night pattern. These rhythmic energy cycles affect your studying as you swing between periods of being alert and feeling dull or slow. Be aware of the "down" times, and you'll avoid hitting the books (and the blahs) when your mind isn't sharp.

Make It an Active Study Break

Chuck was getting ready for the GMAT. He used his breaks between study periods to polish his car. He got pleasure from the activity and at the same time released a lot of physical tension. He was then able to study with more focus and concentration. Chuck passed his exams, and got the added bonus of praise from his friends and even strangers for having "the shiniest car in town."

When you are actively studying be sure to schedule periodic study breaks. These are the brief times when you give your mind a rest and "recharge your batteries." Plan a "non-think" activity like walking, biking, jogging, dancing, or practicing your favorite basketball shots.

Taking a physically active break has many benefits. It builds your endurance and that's a plus on any test, regardless of whether it's a long or short one. Not too many students are aware that stamina is an important part of getting higher grades. If your body and brain poop out too soon, you won't have enough energy for the last parts of the test. There will be no way for you to finish strongly.

In addition to everything else, physical activity keeps your mind and body in balance; your mind won't get exhausted from studying while your body remains primed for energetic movement. Then, when it's time to go to sleep you won't lie in bed with your muscles tensed, ready for action and "vibrating," while your mind races in circles and you wonder why you can't relax.

MEMORY TECHNIQUES

Memory techniques have been in use for centuries. Many, such as the P.E.G. System described below, have withstood the tests of time. Others that follow are more recent innovations. Students universally find they work really well for enhancing memory. Use the ones that do the job for you and discard the rest.

The P.E.G. System

This is an up-to-date edition of a memory tool that originated during the time of the Roman Senate and before the birth of Christ. It involves pairing facts with images and then linking the images so that remembering one brings up its associated other.

The way it works is very simple. A Roman orator might imagine various parts of the room or arena in which he would be speaking. He might start at one side of the room and continue to the other side, noting statues, columns and arches, and the order in which they appear. He would then peg key thoughts to each item.

At the time of his speech, he had only to let his glance proceed from statue to column to arch. In this way he could recall his points in the order in which he wanted to make them. Each feature in the building provided a memory jogger he needed to bring the necessary key ideas to mind. Used this way, the P.E.G. System allowed for a smooth and uninterrupted presentation.

In its present version, P.E.G. stands for **(P)** Pictures, **(E)** Exaggerate, and **(G)** Glue. The picture is the image you create. It is what ties the idea or fact to a subject or object. You make the picture more memorable when you exaggerate it; the more bizarre, the better. The glue is the action you apply to the unique images you have created. Putting your images in motion helps "stick" the facts and ideas into your memory.

The P.E.G. system works because it relies on the right hemisphere of your brain, the part that is creative, makes images, and sees things in an overall and interconnected way. According to current research, the more gaudy, fantastic, and active you make a visualized image the more likely you are to remember it. So, use lots of creative "glue" to exaggerate and enhance your visualizations. Most of all, have fun as you improve your memory!

Just as a Roman speaker did, when you recall a progression of images the facts connected with them will come to mind. You can use specific items in the classroom where you will be taking the test. You could also create a series of images based on anything you choose, either real or fantasized. The images should be as vivid and contain as much detail as possible. Add bright colors and wild patterns, and exaggerate the elements in any way you can.

The Old Elephant Trick

For a bit of practice, use your imagination to visualize a pink elephant. It has long black eyelashes, a blue polka-dot bow on its head, and toe nails painted red, white, and blue.

Now connect something you want to remember to the elephant. Perhaps you see the information painted on a sign astride its back or being towed on squeaky little wheels behind the animal. Maybe you imagine a number of fanciful elephants, all connected to each by their trunks and tails, just as you've seen in old circus posters. Use your imagination to enhance the images with more design, color and action.

If you were studying for a political science exam you might see the elephant with its trunk hooked to the tail of a red donkey. The donkey is wearing red and white stripped pants and a blue stovepipe hat and carrying a sign on which you have written the important facts you want to remember. Make the image even more elaborate by adding more elephants or other elements.

Link 'Em Up

Always strive to link the parts in some unique manner. Perhaps the elephant is riding a tricycle or the donkey is astride a Harley . You might imagine them connected by a flexible, striped bungee cord. Elaborate the images in any way you choose. The idea is to have fun, and give your imagination free rein to come up with truly "rememberable" visual images.

You can peg images to anything, including your own body. After all, your body is the one object that always travels with you regardless of where you go. Simply start with your feet and work upward, or start with your head and work downward. Peg images or facts to various parts of your feet, ankles, shins, legs, torso, etc. Visualize the body part and "connect" it to a fact, formula, date or whatever. Your body can be used for linking material from any number of different subjects.

Using the P.E.G. System

The system can be useful for everyday activities as well as for school. Suppose you needed to remember a shopping list for a picnic you were planning. Here's how P.E.G. might help you do it.

Imagine yourself at the neighborhood market. Get a cart and start down the aisles. The first item on the list is mayonnaise. As you pick up the jar the lid comes off and mayonnaise spills over your bare feet. You can feel the cold, slimy, slippery mess between your toes as you walk.

The next item is mustard. Paint a band of yellow mustard around each knee. Ice cream is on the list, and as you lift the carton the bottom falls out and the ice cream drops onto your pants. You can feel the coldness on your thighs. Some may even have found its way inside your waistband.

You then go to the meat counter for fresh hot dogs, the kind that come linked end to end. Selecting a dozen or so, you tie them around your waist like a belt.

Going to the bakery section, you get a package of hot dog buns. There are eight buns per package, so you put one bun on each finger. You need relish and after choosing your favorite brand, paint a stripe of relish on your shirt, down the middle of your chest. Napkins are important on a picnic, and you place a pile of napkins on each shoulder as though they were epaulets. You find cups in the same aisle and place one over each ear as though they were earphones. The last item on this list is soft drinks. You look up and see a variety of sodas hanging from strings attached to the ceiling. Pluck off a few and drop them into the basket. It is time to go to the checkout stand.

Now write down the shopping items without referring to the paragraphs above. Don't be surprised if you remember every item in order. Notice how your body worked to enhance your memory. Beginning with your feet, you used different parts of your body and tied images to them. Using your five senses helped make the visualizations more real and believable.

The Pegboard System

This memory technique is a fairly recent adaptation of the P.E.G. System. It doesn't relate ideas or facts to objects in the room, your own body, or an imagined group of items. The Pegboard System uses a memorized list of nouns or pegging words that rhyme, whenever possible, with a set of numbers called the stimulus words. You couple these stimulus words with items you want to memorize. You then create an exaggerated image of both the words and items to implant them firmly into your memory.

Researcher A. Paivio found that the stimulus word functions as a sort of "peg." Ideas or facts associated to the stimulus word becomes "hooked" during learning periods. When it's time to recall information, the peg or stimulus word brings the material to mind. According to Paivio and many other researchers, the more concrete and vivid the stimulus, the more "solid" it is as a conceptual peg, and the better the recall.

Pegboard Words

The list of pegging words is fairly standard. It's the images you create that make the Pegboard work. Much like the original P.E.G. System, the more interesting and unusual the images, the better will be your memory. You can create your own list of words as long as they can be matched to the numbers they represent. Words that rhyme with the numbers are even better. The following list is a good beginning:

1.	Bun	6.	Sticks	11.	Raven	16.	Soccer team
2.	Shoe	7.	Heaven	12.	Elf	17.	Sack of beans
3.	Tree	8.	Gate	13.	Earth	18.	Crate
4.	Door	9.	Sign	14.	Forest	19.	Fire scene
5.	Hive	10.	Hen	15.	Fire	20.	Money

Using the Pegboard System

The best way to use the Pegboard System is with a two-step approach.

❶ Memorize the pegging words, either those shown above or words you create, and their associated numbers.

❷ Pair the items of information you want to remember with the pegging word(s) you've already memorized.

Use one pegging word for each fact or piece of information. When you recall the number and its pegging word, it will quickly bring the connected material to your mind.

For example, you can learn and memorize the astrological signs of the Zodiac using the Pegboard System as follows:

No.	P.E.G.	Item	Mental Image
1.	Bun	Aries (Ram)	A **ram** leaping in the air with a hot dog **bun** on each horn
2.	Shoe	Taurus (Bull)	A **bull** wearing floppy tennis **shoes**
3.	Tree	Gemini (Twins)	**Twin** colored gemstones stuck in the trunk of a **tree**
4.	Door	Cancer (Crab)	A **crab** at the front **door** holding a can of Canada Dry in its pincer
5.	Hive	Leo (Lion)	A **lion** running from a **hive** full of angry bees
6.	Sticks	Virgo (Virgin)	A young girl named **Virgin**ia is playing pickup **sticks**
7.	Heaven	Libra (Scales)	**Liber**ace playing the **scales** on a piano in **heaven**
8.	Gate	Scorpio (Scorpion)	A **scorpion** opens a **gate** with its tail.
9.	Sign	Sagittarius (Archer)	The **archer** fires an arrow into a **sag**ging bullseye painted on a **sign**
10.	Hen	Capricorn (Goat)	A **hen** wearing a **cap** rides on the back of a **goat**
11.	Men	Aquarius (Water Bearer)	A group of **men** drinks from a **water** jug carried by a young woman named **Aqua**
12.	Elf	Pisces (Fishes)	An **elf** wearing a coat made of brightly colored **pieces** of cloth sits by a stream, **fish**ing

The Pegboard System is easy to learn, fun to use, and requires only periodic practice to remain effective. You'll be amazed at how long the images you create will stay in your memory, and how easy they are to recall.

Acronyms: Linking Elements Together

An acronym is a word formed by the first letters of othe words. It's used to link concepts and elements. A one word acronym often substitutes for a complete sentence. For example, NATO is an acronym that quickly identifies the North Atlantic Treaty Organization. You don't need help knowing what organizations the acronyms FBI, IRS, and CIA refer to.

Adding humor when you create or link acronyms is a definite plus. Try coming up with an unusual or even bizarre scenario that includes all the organizations just listed. One possibility: The FBI has asked the CIA to spy on the IRS. It boggles the mind that the idea of that reality is so absurd, yet so possible in our politically complex system of government.

An acronym should be easy to remember, and works best when it is a familiar word that ties different elements together. A quick example: Suppose you needed to remember the three stages of memory processing. These are: (1) Acquisition or Encoding, (2) Memory Storage, and (3) Memory Retrieval. Your sister's name just happens to be Esther. You can use her name as an acronym to help you memorize the three stages as follows:

E	=	**E**ncoding or Acquisition
St	=	Memory **St**orage
he**R**	=	Memory **R**etrieval

Acronyms work well when you need to remember numbers. The key is in the way you arrange them. Consider the following groups of numbers, each of which contains nine digits:

900490306   564775829   8003624777

Rote memorization of a list of numbers such as these would be a difficult chore. However, if we add hyphens in strategic places the numbers become much easier to work with and learn.

90049-0306   564-77-5829   800-362-4777

Zip Code   Social Security   Telephone Number

You encounter social security numbers, zip codes, and telephone numbers almost every day. They're usually presented in a certain format. You can use these well-known arrangements, with the included hyphens, to firmly set the numbers into memory. It's one more way to make it easy for you to remember and recall them.

Pace Yourself

Learning to pace yourself can be a great advantage in any study program. Here's a schedule that works well: Study for 45 minutes and then take an "active" 15 minute break. "Active" means really doing something physical. Taking active breaks is an opportunity for you to burn off physical energy to equalize the mental energy used as you study. The idea is to stay balanced in both mind and body. Exercising your body-muscles allows your brain-muscle to get a good rest.

Visualizations that Help

The following group of visualizations are presented because students seeking to improve their memory skills have found them very helpful. If the images seem strange, suspend your judgement and just go with them. See which work for you.

❶ As you read your textbook, imagine that light beams extend from your eyes to the page. See the words or symbols lift off the page and come up to you, traveling on the beams of light. They move from the page to your eyes, and from your eyes the words channel to your brain. When you need to recall the information, you can visualize it leaving your brain and passing through your eyes onto light beams that carry the sentences down to the page in front of you.

❷ To eliminate outside distractions, imagine you are viewing the words on the page through a hollow tube, much like the tube from a roll of paper towels. Visualize the information traveling up the tube, through your eyes and into your mind, undisturbed by any outside interference. When you're in the middle of an exam and you need to recall what you've learned, imagine the information traveling from your mind back down the tube and onto the paper. Then all you have to do is write it down.

❸ Studies have shown that we most easily recall what we find to be interesting. Think of how well you know the words to your favorite song and how easily they come to mind. See the images that occur in your mind as you think of the words to the song. The same thing can occur when you study. Discover the intriguing elements found in any subject or course.

❹ Each time you prepare to study, take a few moments to relax and close your eyes. Allow the following image to appear to your mind's eye. See yourself seated at the table with the material neatly laid out in front of you. Note how concentrated and focused you are on the pages. Notice how easily the words, sentences and paragraphs come to you.

With each breath, your body can become more relaxed even as your mind grows more alert. You can visualize the information flowing to you more and more easily. You can see yourself feeling calm, peaceful, and alert. Now, having programmed yourself, stay in this relaxed state, open your eyes, and begin to study.

❺ When it's been a rough day and your mind seems overly cluttered with thoughts and problems, it can be a real chore just getting yourself to think clearly enough to study. Try the following enjoyable and crazy little experience that was first used successfully with autistic children in San Francisco.

❻ Visualize yourself standing in front of a large sink. Now see yourself literally opening the top of your head. Notice how your skull is hinged at the back. Take out your confused and tired brain that is so jammed full of stuff. Gently wash away any unnecessary or unneeded junk and debris. Watch the old "dirt" flow down the drain. When your brain is freshly bathed, return it to your head. Close the top of your skull and pat your hair neatly back into place. Now your brain is clean, uncluttered, and ready to work for you. There's plenty of room for new information.

ADDITIONAL STUDY HINTS TO USE

Some of the following tips may seem silly or even a bit bizarre. However, they work and according to students, quite effectively.

Study Out Loud

When you study, adding the sound of your own voice to the words your eyes are seeing is an easy way to improve memory and recall. This may sound silly but it is absolutely true. Hearing yourself as you say the words helps improve your memory retention. Reading notes out loud increases the amount you remember by a substantial amount, somewhere between twenty five and one hundred percent. To make your review even more productive, add muscle memory by speaking your notes aloud as you write them. You'll find this a particularly efficient method for learning a foreign language. Of course, if you are shy, this is one technique you may wish to do only when you are alone.

Short Bursts is Best

You learn better when you limit each study period to 45 or 50 minutes. Couple the study period with a 10 to 15 minute activity break (see Cycles and Rhythms, above). Research has repeatedly shown that one-hour sessions spread over a few days are much more effective than a mind-numbing four-hour bout. Studying in short periods allows information to build on itself and to become integrated with what you learned earlier. It is the difference between building your memory little by little, and trying to stuff it full in one shot. Now you know why last minute cramming doesn't work, no matter how much midnight oil you burn.

Play Teacher With a Friend

Work with a friend who is as good a student as you, and one who knows more than you is even better. Ask each other questions you think might be on the test. Cover as much territory as you can, focusing on questions you know will be on the test and those you don't expect to see. Write down the questions and answers both of you come up with and use this list as a final review. You'll be amazed at how many of the questions appear on the exam.

MINING YOUR MEMORY

Tying a string or bandage around your finger is a time-honored way to remember something.

Unfortunately, sometimes not even a good string works. Then, you have to find another way to retrieve that lost information from your mental memory box.

Almost everyone has a special drawer or box where they put stray and odd items they don't want to part with but aren't currently using. It's much the same when you want to remember something, but can't quite bring it to mind. That is when it's "on the tip of your tongue" and will drive you crazy until you remember it. The following strategies work great for retrieving memories from the "lost box" in your mind. As with all suggestions you'll find in NO MORE TEST ANXIETY, check them out and use only those that do the job for you.

Repeated Repetition

Rehearsals strengthen and reinforce memory. Ongoing repetition is an essential memory technique. The process is best explained as practice, practice, practice. Sports fans are a wonderful example of the process in action. Whether their interest is baseball, football, basketball or soccer, true sports fans eat, live and breathe their passion. Aside from attending games whenever possible, they talk with other fans to compare games and statistics, argue about particular players, and remember memorable moments. They fully focus on their sport and are eager to learn more about it. They want information and seek it out.

Finding the Key to Your Memory Box

Missing facts can be retrieved even when you are in the middle of a test. When you know you kept something but don't quite remember where, a good place to begin searching is your personal memory drawer or box. It's the place in your mind where you store lost thoughts and ideas.

Most importantly, don't lose your cool or your concentration. When you have trouble remembering an important fact during a test and get anxious, you'll only push the needed information farther from your conscious awareness.

Stay relaxed and remember that the key to finding lost facts is in your head. Use any retrieval strategies you can to find the answer. Attempt to picture the item or to sound it out. Think of similar or connected material that might bring the item to the surface. Visualize the page of notes that included the item, or picture the words.

Whatever you do, so long as time permits, do not give up. Keep searching through your mind's lost-and-found-box. You committed the information to memory, and it's definitely there.

SUMMING UP

Good study skills are absolutely necessary if you're going to perform at your peak and get the grades you deserve. In Step 7: Test Wiseness, you'll learn the techniques that let you show your stuff, and earn the high test scores you may not have thought possible.

Step 7: Test Wiseness

Scoring High...
At your best when you take a test

This chapter introduces the art of being test-wise. The vast majority of students don't realize that, when they take a test, their grade depends on two very different kinds of "knowing."

The first and most obvious "knowing" a test measures is your understanding and fund of information about a subject. The second "knowing" is seldom thought of or considered. It is, very simply, what you know about taking tests. Knowledge of your subject isn't enough to guarantee a good grade. You must also know how to respond to a test the way the test is designed. This chapter presents useful techniques you can use with different types of tests, from essays to multiple-choice and most everything in between.

GENERAL TEST TAKING TECHNIQUES

Let's say that two students have the same fund of knowledge about a subject. Guess which student will get the higher grade if one is test-wise and the other is not. You're getting the message: Any test measures not only what you've learned, but also what you know about taking tests.

Test-Wiseness

Being test-wise enables you to earn higher grades. It also gives you confidence that comes with knowing you can successfully take tests. All by itself, self-confidence reduces unnecessary anxiety. A test-wise student will score higher than students who may have learned the same information, but are not versed in the "how-to-do-it" of test taking.

Test-wiseness is defined as a student's capacity to use the characteristics and formats of the test and/or the test-taking situation to receive a high score (Millman, J., Bishop, C. H., & Ebel, R., 1965). Being test-wise means knowing how to respond to different test formats and testing situations. When you can do that consistantly, you'll achieve higher test scores.

You may be one of those fortunate few who have an intuitive understanding of tests, and have a "gut" knowledge of the ways in which different tests are put together. No doubt you found your built-in awareness valuable. You probably also realized you did better on tests than many of your fellow students, and you were able to get a higher score with less effort. They may have appeared brighter or smarter, but your grades were either right up there with theirs or even higher.

For many students, being test-conscious is not so easy. As with any talent, some students are naturally test-wise. They don't need to exert extra effort to understand how a test is put together. For those who are not test-taking naturals, learning test taking skills is much the same as learning study skills.

Developing Strategies

Tests are constructed to gauge different kinds of knowledge. Test-wise students are able to develop effective strategies for taking particular kinds of tests. They recognize that each test has its own characteristics and form, and that all tests have relevant and not-so-relevant task keys. These are the built-in hints that help a test-taker know how to best approach the questions.

Test-wise students answer questions the way the person who constructed the test wants them answered. They make use of any consistent patterns in the test to distinguish correct from incorrect answers. They will guess wisely when there is no penalty for guessing. They don't second-guess themselves. They work as quickly and as accurately as time permits. These and other test-taking skills will be covered in the rest of this chapter.

Anxiety's Effect

Excessive worry impacts test-wiseness. Highly test-anxious students have a difficult time recognizing the most advantageous ways to take a test, because they are preoccupied and concerned about doing badly or failing. They don't realize that excessive worry can cause informational keys to be misinterpreted. So much of their attention is directed inward toward negative thoughts and being emotionally upset, that they overlook important information. Too often, distracted thinking leads them to unnecessary errors and unanswered questions.

BE PREPARED

The Boy Scouts had it right. You had to be prepared when you went into the woods. And, when it comes to tests, you have to know the material. The most important test-taking skill you can have is a thorough knowledge and understanding of the material that will appear on the test. Not knowing the information on which you will be tested makes all the test-taking skills in the world absolutely useless. Here's where you learn that the type of test you will be taking determines the best study methods to use as you prepare for the exam.

What's the Test Format?

The way you study for a test depends upon the kind of test you'll be facing. Will the exam be multiple choice, essay, true-false, fill-in, matching, short answer, or a combination of everything? You need to know.

For instance, multiple choice tests require you to recognize a large number of related items. That doesn't mean you have to know everything about each item or fact, just that you are able to recognize them in relationship to each other. In an essay exam you need to produce general information backed up by a few specific facts. Short answer, true-false and fill-in-the-blank tests require as many specific facts and details as possible.

If this is your first test in a class you can ask the instructor what test formats to expect. Another source of information is students who have already taken the course. If that sounds slightly shady, be advised: There's nothing illegal or unethical about getting filled in on the format of the tests you'll be facing.

Whenever possible, check out past tests. They often provide valuable clues about possible test content. Past tests also indicate specific content-areas emphasized by the instructor. These same test areas might be included in the next test. They definitely deserve special interest.

Read the exam with an objective and critical eye. Ask yourself questions such as:

- Are facts favored over ideas?
- Is the emphasis on major ideas or on trivia?
- Are the questions abstract or concrete?
- Is the wording straight forward, or is it designed to trap or trick you?
- Does the instructor focus on details?
- What are the instructor's attitudes about tests?
- What kind of test does the course itself suggest?

The important thing is to "think" test-wise. Asking questions such as these puts you in the same general frame of mind as the person who created the test. It helps you anticipate the test format and make reasonably accurate guesses about different questions that might be included.

Know the Instructor

Knowing your instructor also provides valuable information you can use to predict the possible format and content of an upcoming test. Keep these points in mind as you consider the following:

- What material did the instructor emphasize during class lectures?
- How did the instructor present the subject matter?
- How detailed did the instructor get when lecturing?
- What were the class goals?
- What was the focus of the assignments?
- Did the instructor display any notable idiocyncracies that point in any particular direction?

It's Smart to Ask

It pays to ask questions. Obviously, you have a better shot at a good grade when you understand what the test will cover. Study after study confirms that students often waste precious time and energy studying material that's unlikely to appear on the exam.

Teachers ordinarily avoid questions about specific test items. However, they are usually more than willingly to define general areas of study and what content the student is responsible for knowing.

Contrary to popular opinion, teacher's evaluations aren't based on the number of students they flunk. Rather, they are judged on the quality of their teaching. It's in an instructor's best interests that you do well.

Don't Hesitate to Get Help

If you give it your best efforts and you still have difficulty learning the material, seek help from your instructor or find a capable tutor. Don't let your frustrations build to the point where you want to give up. You'll be psyching yourself out of a chance to do well. Be cautious about deciding that trying is too much effort. It's when you "know" you can't learn the material no matter how much energy you spend that you've lost the battle. Don't admit defeat before you've given yourself a fighting chance.

Frustration that comes too quickly can also be an indication of an undiagnosed learning disorder. Learning disabilities require assistance from a trained professional. If you do have a learning disorder, an educational therapist can help you find ways to use your strengths and minimize any deficiencies. See Appendix A for information about learning disorders and how to identify them.

LOOK AT TEST-TAKING FROM ALL SIDES

Approach tests from a holistic point of view. As you learned in Step 6, you need to have good physical, emotional, and mental balance in order to perform well. In many ways, every test is a combination of chess and a horse race. Tests measure not only the learning you've acquired, but also your staying powers, ability to formulate and use good test strategies, and how well you manage time.

It's a Horse Race

Overall physical and mental fitness should be more than a before-the-test concern. Fitness and stamina influence all areas of your life. You cannot boost them "on demand" the day before a test.

Keeping fit needs to be a year-round activity, with part of your daily routine being a focus on regular exercise and proper diet.

Establish schedules for study, class, and work that permit healthy eating and sleeping patterns. Athletes know that a proper training schedule must include wholesome, energy-producing meals and enough restful sleep to replenish their energy. Without these necessary ingredients, they will not be able to perform at their best. The preparations you make for any upcoming test are no less important. Rest and good nutrition have a direct, positive effect on your test scores.

It's vital that you be physically rested before beginning a test. Numerous research studies demonstrate that taking a test while tired from lack of sleep or emotional upset is an almost sure bet for a poor grade. Diminished thinking and fatigue go hand-in-hand. You simply cannot think clearly when you're physically tired or emotionally drained.

Where's It Being Given?

This is one area where leaving things to the last minute can cost you a bundle, and procrastinators have a tough time. Very simply, if the test is being given at some place with which you are not familiar, be sure to check out the route and the exact location before the big day. You're not going to feel relaxed rushing from place to place, trying to find a building or classroom while the clock ticks off the minutes toward the starting time. Just thinking about it can cause your anxiety level to climb.

Be Early

Along with knowing where the test will be given is getting there a little early. In all probability, you will begin any important test feeling a bit uptight. Remember, a little anxiety is a good thing because it keeps you more alert. Controlling your anxious feelings on the day of a test begins before you enter the testing room. Arriving early can be very helpful. You're certain of being on time, you have an opportunity to collect your thoughts, and there is less chance of getting into a panic before the test even begins.

Making good use of the period before an exam starts is also part of being truly test-wise. You can take those deep breaths and use auto-hypnosis to put yourself into a relaxed, yet alert, test-taking frame of mind. Get yourself accustomed to the surroundings, particularly if this is not your usual classroom, and prepare to concentrate and focus by tuning out any possible distractions.

Pick a seat you like, one that insures you will have enough light for good, effortless vision. Straining to see in some dark corner of a room won't do much for clear thinking or your eye muscles. At the same time, think about siting away from the window and its enchanting, though distracting, views.

Dress for the Occasion

Caroline spent months preparing for her clinical psychology oral licensing exam. She had already passed the written test and this was the final hurdle. A pass meant having her license as a mental health professional. The exam took place in a modern, air-conditioned building on a warm spring day in May. Caroline went into the examination room and said it felt as though she had entered a frozen food locker. She swore she could see steam rising from her breath. Sitting in the cold room, her thinking became as slow moving as frozen Jello. You can guess the results.

The end of this story is a lesson in learning from your mistakes. Caroline took the orals again six months later. Yes, she passed. And yes, she had a warm sweater with her the second time around, just in case.

Simple comfort can make a tremendous difference in your ability to perform. When you visit the test location before the test, notice the room's temperature and plan to dress accordingly. This is one area where preparation has a huge payoff.

Remember the Goodies

If it is a long test, don't forget bottled water and a snack to keep you going at peak level. Avoid anything too sugary; the boost you get will be quick but short lasting, and the energy fall-off is usually quick and substantial. A banana, power-bar, trail mix or granola snack will provide you with more sustained energy.

The night before the exam pack your pencils, pens, erasers, your calculator, or whatever else you anticipate needing. Once you find a comfortable place to sit, arrange your goodies so they're close at hand. All this attention to details is for your personal comfort. The little extra effort goes a long way toward moving the odds for a higher grade in your favor. Best of all, you'll know you're ready and prepared, and that is a terrific confidence builder.

Be Time Wise

Dick, a high school student, was diligently working his way through a section of the SAT when suddenly a voice announced that only ten minutes remained. *Panic!*

Dick said when he heard the announcement he froze. With his heart pounding, Dick looked at the page and saw the large block of unanswered questions. All he could think of doing was to roar through the remainder of the test and guess as best he could. With so little time remaining, Dick barely read the questions and marked the answers in a completely helter-skelter fashion.

Dick forgot a cardinal rule of wise test-taking. *Never forget the clock.* Taking a test this way is like using "The clock doesn't count" system. It's almost guaranteed to get you into trouble, and earn you a lower score. On the other hand, if you're the type who plays poker and always seems to get your card when drawing to an inside straight, this strategy might work quite well. Fortunately, for the rest of us, another much more successful solution is available.

Using Time Effectively

Achieving the highest score possible is a matter of making the clock your ally and using time to your advantage. It only makes sense for the majority of your time to go toward earning the greatest amount of credit. One way to do this is by dealing with the easy questions first, the more difficult second, and the really time consuming questions last. The idea is to take advantage of your strengths to earn "easy" credits, quickly.

This little system is guaranteed to get you the most amount of credit in the least amount of time. Saving the difficult questions for last is smart time management. It makes no sense and is very inefficient to start at the first question on an exam and plow straight through, one by one, to the end. The odds are too big that you won't get to the last questions before the clock says "time's up."

Too often, highly test-anxious students get "hung up" by the clock. To avoid answering questions wrong they compulsively check and recheck their answers. They'll keep checking even when they know they're running out of time. At the other extreme are students who become obsessed about the time remaining. These students waste time repeatedly checking the clock. This increases their worry and fear that they won't be able to finish in the allotted time.

Put It In the Bank

Here's another way to look at getting the most score when taking a timed test:

Earning credit on a test is comparable to the way you build a savings account. Answering a test question or solving a problem is much the same as putting money in the bank. Every correct answer is an addition to your account. Obviously, it pays to build your account as fast as you can.

First, quickly scan the exam. Answer the questions you are absolutely sure of, the ones you know almost without having to think about them. Since you know them cold, answering these questions is like salting away easy money. Deposit each correct answer to your account.

Be careful! If this is a multiple-choice exam, don't lose easy credit by being careless. Take a few seconds to make sure you've marked the answers in the correct place on the score sheet. Also, if you have changed an answer on a scantron or other machine-scored answer sheet, make sure you carefully and completely erase any marks that you don't want there.

Second, put a small circle next to questions you have doubts about, but are still fairly certain you know. These are the questions where you feel the answer or solution is just out of reach, hidden some place in your mind. Put a check mark next to questions or problems you simply do not understand or about which you don't remember anything at all. Also put a check mark next to any item that is taking too much time for you to answer or solve. In each of these cases, leave the question and move to the next. You will come back to the marked questions later.

Third, go back to the items marked with a small circle. These are the questions that may require some extended thinking and/or problem solving. The chances are, you were jogging your memory as you read through the exam and answered the easy questions. You can now more easily recall the information that was on "the tip of your tongue." Deposit the credit for answering these questions into your account.

Fourth and last, approach the questions marked with a check. These are the questions that seemed most difficult when you first read them, the ones you expected would take the longest time and involve the greatest effort. The item may be a problem that turned out to be more difficult to solve and was more time consuming than you anticipated.

Spend whatever time remains working on the tough items. Answering any of them correctly is like earning extra interest in your savings account. So, if there is no penalty for answering a question wrong and your grade reflects only the number of correct answers, the last few minutes are the time to make educated guesses.

Give Your Memory a Break

Suppose you are about to take a chemistry test and you're afraid you'll forget the formulas you need to know. Obviously, your first choice would be to go into the exam with everything written on a sheet of paper. Since that is usually a no-no, the next best choice is to write the formulas on the test booklet as soon as the test has begun. Once that's done, you can concentrate on the exam, and not on being anxious or worried about forgetting the information.

This little tip is also good for history dates, math formulas, or getting down those key words that can trigger your memory for the answers you need to know.

A Small Note of Caution

Here are two points of caution when taking objective tests:

❶ Avoid marking and passing too many questions in search of the easy ones. Rereading questions too often takes time away from answering them.

❷ Don't second-guess yourself. Unless you have a good reason, changing answers on a test will result in wrong responses more often than right ones. As a rule, your first answer is probably a good response and comes directly to you from your instincts or unconscious knowledge. On the other hand, if you firmly believe you should change an answer, do it. Clues will very often pop into your consciousness, or some word may nudge your memory as you progress through other questions on the test.

Helpful Time Strategies

■ Make time your friend. Take a brief moment at the beginning of the test to figure the amount of time you can spend on each test section. Apportion your time so you earn maximum credit for each minute spent answering a question or solving a problem. Spend more time on questions that score at a higher value and less time on the others. An easy example: any question that counts for half the score on a test is worth half the allotted time.

■ On many course tests all questions have the same value. Divide the total time allowed, by the number of questions on the exam. You'll arrive at the amount of time you have available for each question.

■ Standardized tests do the time allotting for you. Each section is timed. You need to be aware of how much time remains before you're told to stop and go on to the next section. Your practice exams should be set up the same way. After doing a few you'll have a good idea of how pacing yourself works. Keep at the practice tests until managing time becomes almost second nature to you.

■ Essay tests require a different strategy. Typically they have a number of different questions and you are supposed to respond to two or three of them. The trick is to read all the questions first. Then pick the ones you can answer most easily . Suppose you know two of them. Write those responses first and then review the remaining questions. By the time you're ready for the third question, your memory may have opened up to the information you need to write on one or more of the remaining items.

■ In every case, use all the time available. When you finish a test early, use the remaining time to check the accuracy of your answers. Double check calculations to be sure you won't suffer the pain of making silly mistakes. Quickly read your answers to be certain you wrote what you intended to write, and so on.

STRATEGIES FOR SPECIFIC TESTS

The tips and techniques that follow are tried and proven. They've been used by hundreds of students, and they work.

Standardized Tests

■ Standardized tests are invariably timed tests. That means you aren't expected to finish all the questions. Use any time saved to review answers to questions you were not sure of, renew your efforts on a question or problems you did not know or couldn't answer, take educated guesses, and check that you filled in the right blanks on the answer sheet.

■ A word about guessing on the SAT-I. The new standardized test includes multiple choice questions in a number of the sections. Unlike the old SAT, the new version now penalizes incorrect answers by 1/4 point when there are five answer choices, and 1/3 point when four choices are offered. The gamble then, is between gaining a full point for picking a correct choice versus losing 1/3 or 1/4 point for an incorrect selection. And, of course, future SAT tests may be different from the version now being used.

Multiple Choice Tests

■ Multiple-choice tests are often an instructor's favorite selection because this type of test is objective and easy to score. Scoring difficulties arise only when a poorly written question (which many often are) is subject to more than one interpretation. Usually, scoring is a simple matter of adding up right answers and, depending on the test format, subtracting wrong ones.

■ These are also the tests that test-wise students like the most, primarily because the questions don't require you to know the exact answer. You only have to be able to identify which choice is more correct, or likely to be more correct, than the alternatives.

■ Within each section on a multiple choice test, questions usually progress from easier to more difficult. Finding an overly easy question toward the end of the section should raise a mental red flag. Read the question again, carefully, and look for some subtlety or trick in the wording.

■ The typical question format is a stem with four or more options from which to choose. An easy example might be:

The fifth president of the United States was

❑ Thomas Jefferson
❑ John Quincy Adams
❑ John Hamilton
❑ Richard Nixon
❑ James Madison

Throw out the obviously wrong answers to increase your odds of picking the right answer from the two or three remaining choices.

■ When you don't know the answer, study the stem of the question and read it carefully. If there are several elements or statements to the stem, be sure you understand each part. Then read all the possible choices. Match the answer you choose against the component parts of the question to see that they all fit. This is particularly important when the choices include "all of the above" or "none of the above." These particular answers must fit every part of the question.

■ An alternate way of approaching multiple-choice questions is to first read the answers before reading the question. One or two of the answers will stand out and simply not fit with the rest of them. You can eliminate these answers immediately. Then read the question. Often, all but one of the answers is wrong no matter how the statement is worded.

■ All or none are absolutes, as are never, every, and always. In contrast, words such as may, often, perhaps, and usually are known as qualifiers. Test-preparers do not want their test answers questioned, so they seldom use qualifiers that might open the answers to interpretation.

■ Be aware that, in most instances, answers containing all, always, never, and none are incorrect. Those words are usually too absolute to be included in correct answers.

■ Very often, the stems and correct answers that appear in class tests have been lifted directly from the text or from notes supplied by the instructor. Here again, knowing only part of the material may be more than enough for you to identify the correct answer. The key is looking at what is familiar. When the question and answer seem to belong together, there's a good chance they do.

■ You can make right choices in one of two ways. The first, obviously, is to know the correct answer. The second is to recognize which of the choices is not the right answer. On multiple choice tests, eliminating the wrong answers is as valuable as knowing the right ones. So, having a little knowledge of the subject can go a long way toward improving your test scores.

The trick is being test wise with what you know. You'll score better than someone who answers the questions randomly. Partial knowledge can raise your overall score substantially.

Great Guessing Versus Just Guessing

Even guessing can be done more expertly.

■ You know that on almost all exams, an unanswered question is considered wrong. So, unless there is a penalty for guessing wrong, marking any answer increases the odds in your favor.

■ Speaking of odds, any multiple-choice question has at least one obviously wrong choice in the answer column. When there are four choices you can usually figure on two clearly wrong items. That cuts the odds of getting the right answer from one-in-four to one-in-two. Using instincts and digging through your memory box will often better the odds substantially. If you simply guessed at the two remaining choices, your chances are at least fifty-fifty. Actually, those aren't bad odds as any gambler would tell you.

■ As you move through the difficult to impossible questions looking for guessing inspiration, one thing you definitely *do not* want to do is tell yourself, "Well, I haven't chosen "b" for a while," or "c" can't be right because I answered the last three questions with "c!"

■ The most frequent mistakes made on multiple-choice tests, and on all other types of tests as well, occur when the test-taker misreads the question or does not follow directions. Work quickly, but make sure you understand exactly what is being asked of you. Then, follow the instructions. Some questions ask for the closest answer, and some for the closest answers. That letter **s** on the end of the word answer is a big clue; don't miss it.

■ READ THEM ALL to be sure you don't miss the most correct answer. If you find that B or D is the correct answer and do not read the rest of the answers, you might miss E, which said both B and D. B was correct, but E was more correct.

TRUE FALSE TESTS

■ Rule number one for true-false tests is never over-analyze. Test creators write true-false tests around facts and details. Much like multiple-choice tests, they generally measure what you can recognize and not necessarily what you must remember.

■ With true-false tests in particular, it's important to read the questions very carefully. Reduce complicated sentences to simple thoughts or phrases. For a question to be marked true, all parts of the original sentence must be true.

■ Be particularly aware when a statement contains two or more independent clauses. When one clause is true while the other is false, you must consider that the entire statement is false.

■ A word of caution: Although you have been warned not to over-analyze, be aware that approximately true may be as close to true as the question permits. If this is the case, mark it as true.

■ True-false tests are usually the "plain Janes" of testing, straightforward and uncomplicated. Some instructors will add ringers in an attempt to make the exam more challenging.

■ Look for absolutes or qualifiers that can change a true statement into a false one and vice versa. Very often, absolute statements are false, since few things in life or school are "always" or "never" the case.

■ Unless wrong answers count against you, guessing is the method of choice for questions you definitely don't know. One hint that can make the job easier: on true-false tests there are generally more questions you can answer "true" because true or positive questions are easier to compose.

■ Instructors are in classrooms to teach the "truth" of a subject. A teacher's natural inclination is to avoid false statements, even those created for a test. Clearly, you can use that little observation to your advantage.

ANALOGIES

■ Word problems, also known as verbal analogies, are often part of standardized tests. They are verbal problems that relate a pair of words together in some way, and ask you to do the same with another set of words.

A simple example is Bird: Airplane = Dog: _____.

Suppose the possible answers are:

        (a) train   (c) sled
        (b) boat   (d) car

■ An effective strategy with word problems is to turn them into sentences. Making a whole thought of the individual words creates a clearer image in your mind. It is much easier to see the relationships when you clarify that "A bird is related to an airplane in the same way that a dog is related to a _____."

Using the choices given above, birds and airplanes both fly by using wings. A dog travels on land using its four legs, one located at each "corner" of its body. Trains move on rails, boats on water, and a sled on snow or ice. The correct answer is (d) car. The reasoning: a car travels on four wheels, each of which is located at a "corner" of the vehicle.

■ Expanding on the idea just given, look for some concept that defines the relationship between the words in the analogy. In the example, the core idea is the way an object, or a part of it, relates to an action.

■ Other useful and often used concepts include:

(1) word meanings

(2) size or amount: large or small, a lot or a little

(3) numerical or verbal sequences: before or after, increasing or getting smaller

(4) part to whole versus part to part

(5) place or location: near to far, height to depth, distance to or distance from

(6) opposites, or things in opposition.

■ Verbal analogy sections on standardized tests are prime areas for guessing. You can help the odds by first eliminating the unlikely answers such as when the word pair presents two different functions or ideas. Generally, you can discard two of the four pairs almost immediately. Your choice then is between two word-pairs, a fifty percent increase in your favor.

VOCABULARY TESTS

Vocabulary tests are a major focus of high school students' attention because they appear on virtually all standardized tests administered to college-bound students. College and university admission departments look closely at vocabulary test results. Their reasoning is that vocabulary is a general indicator of acquired knowledge and thus a gauge of how well the student will do in a demanding college environment.

A very common format involves having the test-taker read a statement or phrase containing the vocabulary word, and then choosing a synonym from four or five choices. In another common format, only the vocabulary word appears along with the choices.

■ Your initial strategy is to read all the answer choices very carefully. Vocabulary tests require recall as well as recognition. It is not enough to simply know the words. You have to work quickly and accurately because vocabulary tests are almost always timed.

■ Vocabulary is one area where practice is essential. Pick up a few practice books and work with them until you can do the word lists quickly and almost instinctively.

■ Very often, the list of choices will include words that sound or look like the root word. Be cautious! Test makers include these "ringers" to confuse or trap the unwary. Watch out for answer choices that are grammatically inconsistent with the root. If the root is a noun, the answer will also be a noun, if it's a verb, look through the choices for a verb.

ESSAY TESTS

Essay tests involve much more than simply choosing a topic, picking up your pen, and writing whatever comes to mind. In fact, successfully answering an essay question begins long before you actually sit down to take the test. From what you write with, to the writing that expresses your concepts, it's attending to the details that will get you a higher grade. Many of the following ideas and suggestions are so evident, you may be surprised they hadn't occurred to you before now.

■ Step number one when doing essays is to choose a writing instrument that feels comfortable in your hand. Do not pick one that is too thin or thick, or requires a lot of pressure to use. You don't want your wrist or fingers cramping up, forcing you to struggle just to finish the test. Find a pen with an easy ink flow that writes without clotting or smearing. It should lay out a track of ink that seems to dry almost instantaneously. Ideally, writing will feel as though it takes virtually no effort on your part.

■ The next step is always to carefully read the instructions. Be absolutely certain about what it is you are being asked to do. Notice the verbs in particular. You don't want to write a great essay and then lose most of the credit because you "explained" when the question asked you to "evaluate," or "described" when you were asked to "discuss."

In case you're not sure of their meanings, here are a few of the common instructional verbs you'll encounter on essay tests.

Compare	Noting the similarities and common characteristics of two or more people, places, or things
Contrast	Examining the differences of two or more people, places, or things
Defend	Justifying and supporting a belief via the use of facts, details, and logical rational
Define	Relate or clarify the basic features of an object
Describe	Inform as to the nature and features of an object
Discuss	Examine a topic or a question and its solutions by logical argument, including different points of view
Evaluate	Assess the worth of an idea or concept, giving the reasons for your solution
Examine	Define and clarify the meaning or essence of a thing
Explain	To make something clear and understandable, or to give the reason for, or cause of some occurance
Justify	Confirm or defend a concept, decision, statement or conclusion

Relate   Describe the association or relationship between two or more persons, places or things

■ You've read the narrative and you're ready to begin writing. Don't! Do NOT simply read the statements, look over the questions, pick the one that seems easiest, check out the clock, and begin to write without thinking any farther. It's virtually guaranteed that this approach is *not* your best tactic for writing good essays.

■ This cartoon of a policeman holding a **STOP** sign is both an image and an acronym. Merely picturing it in your mind will slow the immediate urge to put pen to paper. You'll greatly improve your essay scores by remembering what the picture really means.

S: **STUDY** the instructions carefully, and understand them completely! Read all the questions before picking up your pen. **SEEK** a question you feel confident about, one where you have all the necessary information to write a good essay.

T: **THINK** about the subject. **TAKE** a moment to jot down key ideas, concepts, facts and details you want to include.

O: **ORGANIZE** your approach with a quick **OUTLINE** that puts the ideas and details in the **ORDER** you want.

P: **PRESENT** your thoughts by **PUTTING** the words onto paper. Refer to the outline to keep yourself on track. When you have finished, **PROOF-READ** what you've written.

■ Studying the instructions should be self-evident. I am amazed by the number of students who lose untold points because they read directions carelessly, don't pay attention to details, or assume they understand rather than knowing for sure.

■ Thinking about the subject and taking a moment to write down your thoughts serves a number of purposes. First, once on paper the ideas and facts are there before your eyes. You don't have to worry about not remembering them. Second, the process of remembering something brings details or other material linked to the item to the surface of your mind. Recalling one fact frequently brings up many more. Third, you'll have an advantage in the choice of essay questions to write about. Getting those few words on paper puts you in a better position to decide which question you can answer most easily.

■ After deciding the question you're going to address, organize an efficient approach to the essay. According to researchers, essay readers focus on content and organization when determining credit. These two areas account for the great majority of your score. Spelling and grammar are not the most important factors, though bad spelling and poor grammar will probably lower your score.

■ Make a fast outline to determine the best order for introducing your points and facts. The outline is a visual plan for presenting your thinking on a subject. It minimizes the chances you'll forget important material you need to include. The outline should be "quick and dirty." Use abbreviations and symbols to get your ideas on the paper as rapidly as you can.

■ Essays generally deal more with ideas than with specific events or situations. Organize your outline in a logical manner that reflects the subject matter you are being asked to focus upon.

■ Historic events are best presented chronologically. You can better address social subjects including people and places by viewing them as though you were an objective and impartial observer. Scientifically oriented essays that include reports on experiments are most often written to reflect the order in which the research or development took place.

Additional Tips for Essays

If you follow **S.T.O.P.,** putting your words on paper is the easiest part of writing an essay. To make the job even more effortless, here are several test-wise tips to keep in mind as you get ready to write.

Write To the Question

■ The easiest way to begin the body of the essay is to restate the general statements contained in the original test question. General statements are the specific questions or conclusions you are expected to write about.

■ When addressing a given statement, write from the broad to the specific. As a rule, support each conclusion or point you make with two or three facts or well-buttressed arguments.

■ For essay tests with questions directed toward the hard sciences, arguments and conclusions supported by factual evidence are usually more believable. They will gain more credit than well presented opinions.

■ More philosophically directed questions ask you to demonstrate the reasoning you used to arrive at your conclusions. This is where brilliantly written opinions, not necessarily backed by facts, can go a long way.

■ With any essay, your writing goal is to successfully answer the question.

First Impressions

■ An old adage states that, "You never get a second chance to make a first impression." The first paragraph of an essay sets the tone for the reader: Don't underestimate its importance. It should introduce and summarize your approach to the subject in a way that attracts and holds the reader's interest.

■ Make the introductory paragraph strong and bold, refer directly to the question, and it will set the stage for the points, arguments and conclusions that follow.

■ Write the first paragraph of your essay flawlessly. It is the reader's initial exposure to your response. Pay close attention to spelling, punctuation, grammar, and *everything*.

Special Words

■ Using certain words helps both your writing and the reader.

Evidence, exceptions, compare, contrast, comparisons, and *arguments* are words that stop the eye and alert the reader to pay particular attention to what is coming next.

■ Special words clearly label your intentions while at the same time focusing the reader's attention. They define and clarify your ideas while making the reader's job easier. In the best interest of your score, make the reader's job as easy as you can.

Longest May Not be Best

■ Length is not the primary factor in earning a high score. Be sure to edit as you go.

■ Continually strive to have an organized, succinct approach. Emphasize important points that buttress your reasoning.

■ Directly answer the question in an organized and well-written approach. You'll score more points with a brief but complete answer than with a wordy paper that goes in endless circles. Writing an essay that buries the reader in an avalanche of words will bury your grade as well. Write in a clearly understood, concise and inviting style. The writing will be easier, and you'll be helping the reader arrive at your conclusions without having to strain.

Ending It Right

■ You began your essay by declaring the major statements or conclusions you were to evaluate, discuss, argue, or whatever. Your essay should end with an effective summary.

■ Like the last lick of an ice-cream cone, a good ending leaves a pleasant taste and satisfied feelings.

■ The summary should be brief. It can be as simple as restating the original topic sentence and recapping the general points.

■ Avoid introducing any new elements. They dilute the ending and leave the reader wondering why you didn't include this new information earlier where it belonged.

Being Done Means You're Not Quite Finished

■ If the bell hasn't rung and time isn't up, take advantage of the time remaining to review what you've written. Reread every question to be sure you've answered completely. This is the time to ask yourself a few pertinent questions:

1   Did you follow your outline or stray off on some tangent?

2   Did you write to the question and stay focused on the topic?

3   Did you provide enough facts to prove each of your arguments?

4   Have you clearly distinguished your opinions from facts?

5   Do your words say what you want them to say?

6   Is your summary sentence clearly an ending or has it become a place to put everything you forgot to include in the essay?

READING COMPREHENSION TESTS

Reading comp tests are typically constructed as a short passage followed by a series of questions. They measure your ability to recognize answers contained in the passage. The test demonstrates how good you are at searching out facts and details, or figuring them out from the information you have just read. That is what makes them a popular format for standardized tests.

Traditionally, you're supposed to read the essay and then answer the questions. Students usually follow these directions, attempting to remember as much of the passage as they can until they've answered the questions. While that may be the most logical approach, it is definitely not the best. "Why?" you might ask. The answer is, because this way of doing the test wastes a great deal of time. Reading comprehension tests are usually timed. Your score depends on how well you use time in answering the questions.

■   The secret to higher scores on reading comprehension tests is to turn the process around; read the questions first and then quickly read the passage. As you find an answer, fill it in and go to the next question. Reading the questions first tells you a lot:

1   You will have some idea of what the essay is about from the very first word.

2   You'll know what you are looking for as you read.

3   When the test asks you to draw inferences or arrive at conclusions based on the material, you will have a better idea of the author's intent and how to arrive at your answer.

■   Read the presenting passage or essay carefully! You have seen this advice before, and I cannot state it too often.

■   Keep the questions in mind as you read the material. Note words such as *but, yet, however,* or *while.* They change the intent or direction of the sentence and shift its meaning or focus.

■   Be advised! Do not skip around or jump to the next passage if the initial passage appears too difficult. The easier essays and questions appear first on most comprehensive tests, so your best strategy is to read the initial passage completely.

■   Research shows that, even without knowing the meaning of some of the words, students still understand much of the material and are able to answer many of the questions. The studies also noted that students who skipped from one passage to another got lower scores because they became confused, lost concentration, and missed valuable clues.

■   Keep your own knowledge or opinions out of the picture. They will get in your way and cost you points. Unless asked to do otherwise, limit your thinking and approach to the words, facts, and ideas presented in the passage. That is what you are being tested on, not about anything else that is not a part of the essay.

■   It always pays to check your answer to be sure it fits the sentence and includes all parts of the question. Then be certain you marked it correctly on the score sheet. You don't want to spend lots of effort getting the right answer only to lose credit for it because you checked or filled in the wrong box.

SUMMING UP

If you needed to improve your test-taking skills before you began this chapter, Step 7 has shown you the hows and wherefores. Any test measures two skills: what you know about the subject, and how to best take a particular kind of test. When you have a good fund of knowledge of the subject and an awareness of how to "read" an exam, you can feel more confident about earning good grades consistently, not just occasionally. This book is all about GETTING GOOD GRADES, and not being anxious while you do it.

The last chapter, Putting It All Together, ties up any loose ends, reiterates essential points, and adds additional, helpful hints.

PUTTING IT ALL TOGETHER

Achieving Your Goals

This chapter brings together everything you've learned in NO MORE TEST ANXIETY. Much like tying the knot in a string that's wrapped around many different bundles, this part of the book joins all the elements into one cohesive package. You'll also find comments, ideas, and some new techniques or approaches that weren't covered in earlier chapters.

INTEGRATING BREATHING AND IMAGING

Relaxation begins with easy, natural breathing. As you have already discovered, natural breathing is the easiest way for you to begin relaxing. Good breathing allows you to "let go" of tension and worry, and that leads to reduced anxiety and clearer thinking.

■ Correct breathing is the fundamental skill on which you build all other relaxation techniques.

■ Send a signal to your body and mind to the coming relaxation experienceby coupling an inner verbal signal with your breathing. Do not underestimate the impact those brief words, LET GO, or I AM CALM, can have on your ability to discharge tension.

Focus attention on your breathing and on your personal signal. As you say it, let go of any negative thoughts and images. Feel your mind begin to relax along with your body.

■ Visualize a peaceful scene. It may be an image of a favorite place you once visited, or a pleasing image you create in the moment. It's difficult to experience tension when your mind is occupied with pictures of beautiful scenery. Continue to hold this image in your mind's eye as your body continues to relax and you achieve a state of calm.

Body Awareness

You have an "optimal zone" in which you can perform at a peak level. A certain amount of anxiety is part of that zone; it keeps your mind sharp and your body ready for action. Learn what your optimal zone feels like and get to know it well.

Test anxiety is insidious. It takes hold before you're aware that it has pushed you out of your optimal zone. One moment you are fine. Then you think of that upcoming test, and in the next moment you're heading for trouble. Your body always seems to know that trouble is brewing before your head is aware of it. Your body gets tight. The butterflies begin. Muscle tension may be your first indication that test anxiety is rearing its ugly head.

At test-taking time, almost every student experiences some degree of anxiety. For most, too much anxiety is the problem. And, if you're not aware of how anxiety feels and your reactions to it, there's nothing you can do to relieve the stress and tension.

REVIEWING

Reviewing for a test is more than merely looking over lengthy notes and class material. Whoever prepared the test looked over the same stuff you did and created questions from it.

Now is when good note taking really counts. You've learned to condense and reorganizing your notes. By the time you begin studying for a final, your notes should be brief, informative, and to the point. Ideally they focus around key-words that condense complete sentences down to one or two-word captions.

As part of reviewing for a test, you'll use one of the most effective review techniques available. You're going to ask yourself questions in much the same way instructors do when they write an exam. In essence, you'll be restating your notes about the material in the form of questions. It's like reversing the process of taking notes in the first place.

■ Take a page of your class notes. They should be in a two-column format (see Step 6). Remember, the left column contains the memory-enhancing "key-words" derived from the wider right column. The right column is where you write a more detailed and extensive understanding of the book and lecture material.

■ Cover the right column so that only the memory-enhancing key-words are visible.

■ Create a question or series of questions for each of the key-words in the left column.

■ Answer the questions as quickly, accurately, and completely as you can. When you have finished a page, uncover the right column and check your answers.

■ Note any key-words you had difficulties with or answered incorrectly. Repeat the process until you clearly understand each clue and can answer the questions correctly.

■ When you can easily answer every question connected to each key-word, move on to the next page and repeat the process. After completing the last page, cover the right column on all the pages and answer the questions associated with every word in the left columns. If you stumble, go back over the particular key you missed and check its expanded notes from the right column.

Think, Think, Think

You have to think about a topic to create questions about it. The very process of going over the material and creating different questions firms your memory. Each time you review facts and details, memory traces of the information get reinforced. The material becomes more firmly established and more available for recall when needed.

Complete the review procedure as described above is almost

like receiving an automatic assurance of a good grade on an exam. You will definitely go into the test feeling more comfortable and less anxious because you know the material is stored in your brain.

Do What You're Asked to Do, and No More

If you're old enough, you may remember a television program from the 1960's called "The $64,000 Question." A contestant named Teddy had a photographic memory and an urge to talk. He was going for the "big bucks" and needed to know the answer to only one more question. Teddy answered it, but included more information than he needed to. Unfortunately, while his answer to the question was correct, what he added to the answer was not. Teddy lost the top prize because he didn't follow directions and did not know when to stop.

■ Doing well on any test begins with following the instructions as they appear on the page. Don't interpret or include anything unless you're asked to do so. You are being tested on specific facets from a course or subject, and adding information not called for will only use extra time, take more energy, and lower your score.

■ Use **S.T.O.P.** to help you organize your thinking and your approach to a test. The brief moments you spend thinking before you answer the questions can pay big dividends by the time you've finished. To paraphrase an old Chinese expression: "Remember to put brain in gear before putting pencil to paper."

■ It is frustrating and makes no sense to work like crazy and see your efforts go down the drain. Misreading or misunderstanding simple instructions, checking the wrong boxes, or not turning the page and missing the last dozen questions on a test can all be disastrous to your score.

This is no exaggeration, and it happens all too often. Anxious students can become so frazzled they practically skip right over an instruction telling them to turn the page. Sam was anxious during the SAT. He didn't hear the proctor tell the group they were to continue working until told to stop. As a result, Sam didn't do the last two pages of a section.

■ Use past tests for practice.Read the questions first and redo the answers. Go over the paragraphs or statements in essay and comprehensive tests and then write new responses.

■ Keep focusing on the subject and any material emphasized

by the instructor. In this way you won't sidetrack your studying into irrelevant and time wasting areas.

■ For all tests, and essay tests in particular, be sure you spot the directional words and understand them completely. Think, and jot down your immediate thoughts to get a quick picture of which question triggers the most recall of facts and ideas. Always write to the point of the question.

■ Become familiar with the terms that define exactly what you are to accomplish. Use any descriptive verbs to define your task and direct your thinking so you can answer the question correctly.

TIME MANAGEMENT REVIEW

Final exams, theSAT or ACT, graduate school entrance exams, medical boards or whatever, you've devoted a great deal of effort to arrive at this point. Now is not the time to procrastinate and fritter away your opportunity to get ready for the upcoming exam.

Capitalize on your available time; it is a non-renewable resource. You're building self-confidence when you use time well. You'll know you are ready for the test and in control of your world. Wasting valuable time leads to panic, last-minute cramming, anxiety, worry and stress.

■ Studying for any exam begins far before the actual test date. Early on, get in the habit of budgeting your time to plan sufficient study and review time for each course or subject.

■ Establish daily priorities and don't forget to include time for eating, sleeping, working and exercising. Remember that every exam is also an endurance test; you must prepare both mentally and physically.

■ When you take practice tests, be aware of the clock or your watch. Check the time at reasonable intervals to:

❶ Gauge your progress,

❷ Develop a quicker work-pattern, and most importantly,

❸ Be sure you've allocated most of your time for the highest valued questions.

■ The number of correct answers on the score sheet determines your grade or score, not the number of difficult questions you attempted to answer or the time spent on each question.

155

■ On any test, focus on earning the most amount of points for the least amount of time you spend answering the questions. Leave the lower valued and the toughest-to-answer questions for your final efforts and the last moments you have before time is called.

An articulate and enterprising senior citizen (he was 87 at the time) relayed this story. As a young boy he came to realize that if he first answered all the questions he knew, and then went back and tackled the ones he didn't know, he always passed his tests. He wasn't sure how he came to this knowledge, just that he was surprised that other kids didn't take tests the same way since his method always seemed to work.

MEMORY AND RECALL

Preparing for tests that may be days or weeks away requires you to retain facts and information. You must mentally store material for extended periods before using it. Once you're done with it, you can let it slide from your memory. What you want then, is a longer form of short-term memory.

When you improve your short-term memory you get the added plus of improving your long-term memory as well. For a clearer idea of the process, visualize your mind as an intricate and very sensitive mechanical storage device. Reviewing, creating questions for yourself to answer, and using your time effectively is a way of fine-tuning, lubricating, and maintaining your personal memory and recall machine.

The following are proven methods for improving both short and long-term memories. Some are general to all students while others are more specific in their approach.

Intend to Remember

You have to want to learn and remember. If the will isn't there, the way is unimportant because no way will work. Learning is the active process of acquiring new information. It is not a passive "sitting back and letting it happen." Face it, you're going to expend a fair amount of energy to get that new material into your brain. If succeeding is important, then any effort is worthwhile.

When your goals are clear, it's easy for you to grasp the need for learning and remembering. At times it may be necessary to remind yourself of the goal, to tell yourself, "I know where I'm going." "I need to concentrate." "I want to learn and remember this material." " I am going to succeed."

Core Material versus Everything Else

It pays to know the difference. Distinguishing core material from the surrounding verbiage is like separating wheat from chaff.

■ Core materials are the key ideas, major principles and theories, while elaborated material includes examples and illustrations.

■ To identify core ideas, think like a journalist. Ask yourself the same five "W" questions a newspaper reporter would: Who? What? When? Where? Why?

Answering these five critical questions is essential to organizing and remembering core ideas. All additional information and descriptions only elaborate and explain the core concepts.

Visualize to Enhance Your Memory and Recall

There are good reasons for the old expression, "A picture is worth a thousand words." Here are a few:

■ Language is symbolic. It's an abstract way to represent complex issues or objects. You'll remember something much better when you memorize it as a concrete and realistic image.

■ Recalling an image is easier than remembering a collection of words. Also, the image triggers and brings up other pictures at the same time. Visualizations act as image-links to material you've already learned.

■ Creating mental pictures uses your brain's right hemisphere which can "see" things in a holistic fashion. Your brain does that best when the subject is one you find interesting or unusual.

■ Becoming emotionally involved with something makes it the focus of your attention and concentration. You can focus more directly on the information you wish to retain.

■ Increased arousal helps you remember information, and to shift it from short-term to long-term memory. In short, when you visualize, you remember things better.

It's Just Another Test

Your attitude toward taking a test strongly influences the score you'll receive. Feeling confident and assured about yourself and your abilities are prime factors in achieving higher test scores. Your thoughts and perceptions about yourself can be positive and self-reinforcing, or negative and self-debasing.

■ Your attitude about any particular test is important. If you see an exam as the major hurdle of life, failure will appear to doom you to a minimal salary, cheap car, discount clothing, and nothing better than beans and hamburgers on your plate. The pressures to do well become overwhelming, and getting a good score will look like climbing the Matterhorn.

■ Too often, students assume that poor results on a certain test will, quite literally, determine their future. Take a clearer view and you'll know that is far from the truth. Compared to all the things you'll do in your life, any test takes up only a small portion of your time and energies.

■ Look at tests in the proper perspective, and realize that no test is the end all or determiner of your success or failure.

■ Your future possibilities are unlimited. They are bound only by your desires and the efforts you choose to put forth.

Take the Test for Practice

Carrie is a graduate student who decided to "sit in" on the doctoral exams at her school. She said she did it "just for the exposure and the practice." Carrie felt the experience would help her be better prepared when she took the exams some three months later.

Carrie had nothing to lose, so she took the tests feeling relaxed, unconcerned, and very much at ease. She laughed when she described how some students were so tense and anxiety-ridden they literally appeared to "vibrate." Carrie admitted she became just as anxious as other students during midterms, finals, and whenever a test was really "crucial."

Imagine her surprise when Carrie got the results of the "practice exams" and found she'd passed every segment. What she had done "for practice" she no longer had to do "for real." Carrie said the experience completely changed her thinking about how to prepare for taking tests.

High School counselors urge most students to plan on taking the SAT or ACT at least three times. There's no penalty for doing so, and the student avoids making that one test too terribly important.

■ Take the first one or two SATs or ACTs strictly for practice and experience. You'll learn what to expect and how best to study for the segments you find the most difficult. It won't cost anything other than your time and some effort, and the experience could prove invaluable when you take the test "for real."

■ Practicing on the actual test puts test-taking in an entirely different light. Obviously, if you take a test for practice and get the score you need as the doctoral student did, it means you don't have to bother taking the test again.

While the above scenario is true for many standardized tests, it clearly isn't possible with class-exams. You don't usually get to practice on a class final exam. However, if you can legally get a copy of a previous final, that will do very well as a base for your studying.

Practice. Practice. Practice.

For many years, teachers and counselors have encouraged students to prepare for tests by practicing test-taking skills. Research with high school and college students demonstrates that familiarity with the test-format is a primary factor in higher test scores. The studies confirm the old cliché that, "Practice makes perfect." That is particularly true for standardized tests, where the emphasis is more on finding creative solutions than in demonstrating rote knowledge of a subject.

I can't over emphasize the importance of being familiar and comfortable with the test format. You'll feel more confident and less like you're at the mercy of someone who's out to get you.

An increase in self-confidence almost always equates to a decrease in test anxiety. When you feel confident, prepared, and "know" that you will earn a good score, you can literally feel anxiety drop away. That is why I suggest that you make up your own practice quizzes as part of preparing for any test.

PRE-EXPERIENCE THE TEST SITUATION

While visualizing is important for enhancing memory and recall, it is also useful when you are preparing for a test. And it is especially helpful for minimizing test anxiety. So, how do you minimize anxious feelings connected to a test you haven't yet taken?

A Mental Preview

History is filled with stories of people who faced their fears, overcame them, and went on to great successes. One trait many of these individuals had in common was their ability to anticipate obstacles. They reduced fear and tension by mentally eliminating the unexpected where ever possible.

You can do the same by previewing each stage of the test in your mind. This single step can eliminate a lot of surprises. You'll also bolster your feelings of confidence and determination.

The following visualization will help you mentally rehearse what you might experience on the day of a test. You're going to "preview" stress-producing moments that can occur. Your goal is learning to "disarm" these periods to keep anxious feelings at an acceptable level during the test.

You may wish to order an audio CD or cassette of the script before you do the exercise (Appendix B). You can also have a friend read the script to you, or tape record the visualization yourself.

Visualizing the Test Day

Make yourself comfortable, and relax in any of the ways that work best for you. Close your eyes, take a few full and satisfying breaths, and let go as you've learned to do. Putting yourself into a state of trance will deepen the experience and make it more real.

See yourself wakening on the morning of the test and notice how you feel. Mildly anxious feelings are fine. Remember, a little anxiety is desirable.

Picture yourself getting out of bed and going through your normal morning routine. Don't leave anything out; make the sequence very real. At any point when you become aware of anxiety intense enough to make you feel uncomfortable, **STOP!**

Begin to take in a full and deep breath of air. As you do so, clench your dominant hand into a tight fist. Maintain the tension in the hand as you inhale. Hold the breath and the fist for a moment. Just before beginning to exhale, let your hand relax totally. Mentally recite the "cuing" phrase you learned in Step 1: Breathing. Release any excess tension from the hand and your body.

On the visual screen in your mind, go to a place that's special, safe, and very comfortable for you. Perhaps it will be somewhere you've visited before, either in reality or in your mind. See and feel yourself in this safe and relaxing place. Experience the scene with all your senses and as fully as you can until you feel calm.

Be aware as your anxious feelings diminish and return to an acceptable level. When you're agaian comfortable, move the image of that special place to the back of your mind. Bring images of the test-day to the forefront of your awareness. Now see yourself at breakfast and then on your way to school or the test location.

As your imaginary journey to the test site unfolds, notice any instances of excess tension or anxiety. When they occur, **STOP!** Take a moment to clench your fist as you did earlier. Inhale fully while holding the tension in your hand, and again bring the image of that special place to the front of your mind. Exhale, and as you do so, repeat your cue phrase. Release the tension in your hand and relax completely in mind and body.

Continue the visualization, seeing yourself as you arrive at the test location, find the room and your assigned seat, and prepare to take the test. This is the point when most test-anxious students feel their tension and discomfort levels rising. See yourself sitting down, closing your eyes for a brief moment, clenching your fist and breathing deeply.

Completely experience the relaxation images until you feel calm. Once again, notice when the excess tension has passed and when you feel ready to continue.

Allow the visualization to progress, repeating the relaxation procedure whenever you feel tensions rising past your point of comfort. Focus on how ready you are to take this test. You've studied in a relaxed frame of mind. You know the subject. You've stored the facts and details in your memory, ready for immediate recall. Information will come to mind as needed. You are prepared, ready, and eager to do your best.

Watch yourself finishing the test and checking your answers for accuracy. Before turning the test in, see the grade you want in red at the top of the cover page. Store the image of the grade in your memory. You know you fully deserve it. See yourself handing in the paper or test-booklet. Feel satisfied and good about your performance.

You are not quite finished with your visualization. Before opening your eyes, imagine yourself receiving a reward for your hard work and strong effort. See the prize you want and imagine yourself enjoying it. Experience it fully after you finish studying and each night before going to sleep. Focus on the feelings of having done very well.

Repeat the same visualization until there are no points where anxious feelings become greater than you find comfortable. The more you repeat the exercise, the more effective and real it will be for you. The affirming feelings from the visualization will carry over into the test. That boosts self-confidence along with comfort.

Make It Positive

Sorry for the old bromide, but it definitely does *not* pay to sow the seeds of your own discontent. It's much more productive to cultivate and nourish the belief that you can and will succeed, regardless of the obstacles. This kind of positive thinking is directly related to how you feel, and your feelings definitely affect your score.

You may find yourself in a class that is not to your liking or an instructor who is less than thrilling, or even one that's nasty. If you going to perform at your best, you need to find something in the course that you like and that can hold your attention. You'll reap big dividends when you can reverse negative thoughts and feelings and find ways to put a more positive slant on difficult situations.

A little searching often reveals the good things any class has to offer, regardless of your initial disinterest or dislike. Focus your energies outward on the task at hand and not inward. Your short term goal is to complete the class with the highest possible grade, and an "up" attitude goes a long way toward easing your worry and minimizing any intrusive thoughts.

Stay Away From Vibrating Friends

Without a doubt, getting together with other students during a test break is one of the most self-defeating thing you can do. The five or ten minute rest rest period between sections on standardized tests is the time when students usually rush to huddle together. They agonize over how others answered this or that question, or talk about the stress of having to take the test at all. If you were anxious before, imagine your feelings after meeting with jittery friends.

Rest periods are for replenishing your stength and calming yourself for the next test section. Let your friends vibrate on their own. *You don't need their anxiety!* Find yourself a quiet, peaceful place where you can keep your mind focused. You want to stay "in the test-taking groove," and not be distracted by anybody else's difficulties or doubts. Besides, no matter what your answers are to questions in the last section, it's done! There's no going back.

Get Out of a Bad Mood

How will you do your best during a test if you are down, angry, or worried. For that matter, how will you remember anything when you're studying if you are upset and not thinking clearly?

Let go of the anger at your roommate or best friend for playing the stereo until the wee hours the night before your exam. Unload the irritation at the roommate who ruined your favorite shirt. An angry confrontation with a loved one is painful at any time; just before a big test it can devastate your grade.

What you put down on the test booklet or paper will decide your score, and being distracted by troubles and concerns isn't going to help at all. It is not what goes on inside that counts; it is how you deal with the upset that can make the difference between a good score and a poor one.

Here's one way of dealing with an unresolved issue:

❶ Imagine yourself putting the problem into a tight container or chest.

❷ Move the chest into a place in your mind where it will be safe and out of the way. You know you can retrieve the chest at any time, but you don't have to deal with the problem that's in the chest right now.

❸ Remember to relax. You know that without tense muscles you can't feelanxiety. The same is true of anger and frustration. Staying relaxed and at ease makes it is almost impossible to be angry. You'll be too calm and peaceful to be emotionally or physically upset.

Convert It

Gary stays in wonderful shape by lifting weights every day. He goes from classes to the gym during his lunch breaks or at the end of the day. Dropping the weights Each time a weight drops to the floor, it lands with a resounding thud, accompanied by a mental picture of whoever or whatever is bothering him.

When really ticked or frustrated, he lifts heavier weights, even more vigorously. Gary finds release in converting his emotional upset into physical action. He said he ends his workouts feeling relaxed, peaceful, and again ready to face the job.

Anger or anxiety is easy to convert into positive action. And any vigorous activity helps to reduce your anxiety. Whether you walk, jog, swim, play ball or ride a bike, you're using energy that's connected to your aroused or upset emotions. Clear your thoughts and feelings by keeping the source of your upset in the front of your mind as you perform your activities.

THE MAGIC PEN

Most of the time, simply having fun is the best way to relax. When you combine fun, relaxation, and a potent test-taking tool, you get a lot more than you might have expected.

The following visualization is useful when you need a special tool in your creative, anti-anxiety, feel good, mental gadget box. The image you create will be a fantasy based on reality.

For the reality-based part, choose a pen that writes easily and feels good in your hand. Buy a new pen, or better yet, use one you already have that has special meaning for you.

For the fantasy part, make yourself comfortable and close your eyes. When you've reached a good level of relaxation, visualize a Magic Pen. See it as completely as you can, its shape, color, and size. Hold the pen in your hand. Imagine the feel of it, and connect the feeling with a relaxed and comfortable state of mind.

Visualize yourself ready to take a test. You know that you might be a bit nervous. Bring your special, Magic Pen to mind. Feel the relaxation that flows through your body as you hold the Pen in your hand. It can help you answer the test questions because this Pen comes with very strong and special powers.

With your mind relaxed and clear, notice how easily you're able to think. Look at a question. Notice how the Pen helps you recall what you need to know. Your thinking flows smoothly and without effort. You feel more at ease, and ready to face and complete the rest of the test.

At any sign of excess tension, take a brief moment to focus on the special writing instrument in your hand. Feel sensations of calmness and relaxation flowing from your hand into the rest of your body. When the tension has subsided, go back to the test. You have studied effectively and all the information you need is stored in your memory, ready for quick retrieval. The Magic Pen is there to help you put the words on paper.

Visualize yourself using the Magic Pen as you take the test. See yourself answering the questions, and feeling very competent and positive about how well you are doing. If an answer does not come readily to mind, simply go on to the next question. Know the Magic Pen will help bring the answer to you shortly. Should you begin to feel excess anxiety, focus again on the Magic Pen until your anxiety level is back to a comfortable place.

Just as you learned in Step 6, answer all the questions you're sure you know. When you've finished with these, go back and answer the questions you weren't sure of or that required some extra thinking. See yourself going back over the test to be sure you didn't miss any questions and that your answers are in the right place on the score sheet or booklet. Feel how easy and satisfying the entire experience can be. When time is called, take a brief moment to put your Magic Pen away so it will be ready the next time it is needed.

SUMMING UP

Test-taking anxiety can be overcome. The most important thing this book can do is help you learn to tap into your own potential skills and abilities. Your brain is probably as efficient as the next person's. You have the capacity to overcome obstacles and gain your goals. All that matters is how your express your inherent talent and potential.

Good luck!

Appendix A
LEARNING DISORDERS

According to Federal Government guidelines, a learning disorder is defined as "...a disorder in one or more of the basic psychological processes involved in understanding spoken or written language." It has been estimated that four to five percent of the United States elementary and secondary school populations have specific learning disabilities.

Anxiety is a common characteristic among students suffering from learning disorders. It is also common among students who suffer from test anxiety. Obviously, by itself anxiety does not indicate an individual has a learning disability. Many more factors must be considered before the diagnosis of a learning disorder can be made.

Individuals with learning disorders can exhibit problems in one or more areas that may include listening, thinking, talking, reading, remembering, writing, spelling, or arithmetic. Learning disorders occur in both psychological and physiological forms. They may involve difficulties in the way the person is able to process visual, auditory, fine or gross motor control, communication, logic, and social interactions.

What to Look For

Learning disorders occupy a broad spectrum of learning problems. Academic difficulties may show up in any of the following ways:

- Poor coordination ■ Difficulty focusing
- Immature behavior ■ Poor memory
- Difficulties seeing differences in shapes and colors
- Trouble making sense of what is seen and heard
- Over-reaction to noise ■ A need to take risks
- Limited vocabulary ■ Disorganized language
- Distractibility ■ Impulsivity
- Difficulty concentrating and focusing on one task
- Poor attention span ■ Indiscriminate reactions

- Hyperactivity   ■ Reverses words and/or numbers
- Disorganized appearance and sense of self
- Poor comprehension and retention
- Slow reader and writer   ■ Frequent spelling errors
- Often frustrated   ■ Poor time management
- Often highly test anxious
- And many other possible symptoms

LDs ARE *NOT* MENTALLY RETARDED

A learning disorder is not an indication of low I.Q. or mental retardation. Individuals with a learning disorder may have normal to above average or superior intelligence. Their difficulties lie in the way they erroneously process information. Much like TV signal interference that causes a wavy, fuzzy, or snowy television picture, incoming or outgoing knowledge can become scrambled as it travels the neural pathways between the brain and the eyes, ears, mouth, or other parts of the body.

It Can be Inconsistent

To complicate matters even more, the disorder may not be consistent. It may be present one day and not the next. Individuals can exhibit real strengths at the same time they struggle with weaknesses. A student may have problems in grade school, do quite well in high school, and suddenly encounter the earlier problems once again in college or graduate school. The disorder may be expressed in one specific area such as English, math, or a foreign language, or it can be multiple and pervasive, and expressed in virtually all areas of a person's life.

It's Also a Social Problems

Learning disordered individuals often have trouble recognizing or distinguishing between subtle nonverbal cues. This causes them social problems such as difficulty meeting new people, working cooperatively with others, making friends, or feeling confident or comfortable in social situations. Their inability to correctly perceive or interpret nonverbal messages can result in self-consciousness and lowered self-esteem. The fact that their problem is a result of incomplete or incorrect processing doesn't help how they feel about themselves. Frustration and anxiety are common responses to both the academic and social problems caused by a learning disability.

Academic Difficulties

Learning disorders can interfere in any number of ways with a person's ability to absorb, remember, retrieve, and use information. Some students with learning difficulties are very adaptable. They have learned to deal with their impairment, often by instinct, by working around the limitations imposed by their particular disorder. For example, a student may have a visual-processing deficit that makes reading O.K., but comprehension difficult. The student might compensate by developing a strong audial memory. Instead of learning by visually reading the words, the student learns by hearing the material. In this way, the student can progress through school in a satisfactory fashion and the learning disorder may not be noticed or addressed.

Comprehensive tests such as the S.A.T., A.C.T., or graduate school entrance exams don't lend themselves to compensating techniques. Since they don't simply measure what has been learned about a specific subject or subjects, these tests bring learning disorders into much clearer focus. It is when preparing for or taking a standardized test that some students first discover they have a learning impairment.

SEE A PROFESSIONAL

In short, there are no hard and fast rules. Every individual with a learning disability is unique. If you suspect you may have a learning disability, *CONSULT A PROFESSIONAL.* You may need to be tested to determine whether or not you have a learning problem, the kind and extent of the disorder, and what you can do about it. A specialist in learning disorders can help identify your strengths as well as pin-point any weaknesses. Good starting places might be the local chapters any of the following organizations:

- The Association of Educational Therapists
  818-788-3850

- Attention Deficit Disorder Association
  800-487-2282
- C.H.A.D.D. (Children with Attention Deficit Disorders)
  305-587-3700
- Clearinghouse on Disability Information
  202-205-8241
- Council for Exceptional Children
  800-CED-READ
- Council for Learning Disabilities
  913-492-8755
- Disability International Foundation
  206-577-0243
- Learning Disabilities Association of America
  412-341-1515
- Learning Disabilities Network
  617-340-5605
- National Center for Learning Disabilities
  212-545-7510
- National Foundation for Dyslexia
  804-262-0586
- National Information Center for Children and Youth with
  Disabilities   800-695-0285
- National Parent Network on Disabilities
  703-684-6763
- The Orton Dyslexia Society
- Your high school or college advisor or counselor

Appendix B

**Learning
Skills
Publications
LLC**

NO MORE TEST ANXIETY (Item 1001........................... $ 17.95
   Includes Basic Audio CD (Item 2001)

Basic Audio CD (Item 2001) .... $ 10.95
   Basic guides for breathing, relaxation,
   auto-hypnosis, and focused studying

Audio Tapes (2) (Item 3001) .... $ 14.95
   Basic guides for breathing, relaxation,
   auto-hypnosis, and focused studying

Audio Tape (Item 3002) .... $ 7.95
   Guides for advanced techniques in relaxation,
   studying, and test-taking skills

CD (Item 2002) .... $ 10.95
   Advanced techniques in self-hypnosis, and
   The Magic Pen visualization

Audio Tapes (2) (Item 3002) .... $ 14.95
   Advanced techniques in self-hypnosis, and
   The Magic Pen visualization

For fastest service call toll-free **800-362-4777** or FAX order form
shown on following pages with mc/visa information. When paying
by check, please allow an additional five days.

REFERENCES

Berstein, D., & Borkovec, T. (1973). *Progressive relaxation training: A manual for helping professions.* Research Press, Chicago.

Boutin, G. E. (1978). Treatment of test anxiety by rational stage directed hypnotherapy: A case study. American Journal of Clinical Hypnosis, 21, 52-57.

Boutin, G. E., & Tosi, D. J. (1983). *Modifications of irrational ideas and test anxiety through rational stage directed hypnotherapy.* America Journal of Clinical Hypnosis, 39(3), 382-391.

Davis, M., Eshelman, E. R., & McKay, M. (1988). *The Relaxation & Stress Reduction Workbook.* New Harbinger Publications, Inc., Oakland, California

Erickson, M. H., (1980). *The Nature of Hypnosis and Suggestion, Volume 1.* Rossi, E. L., Editor, Irvington Publishers, Inc., New York, N.Y.

Erickson, M. H. and Rossi, E. L. (1976). *Hypnotic Realities.* Irvington Publishers, Inc., New York, N.Y.

Fanning, P. (1988). *Visualization for Change.* New Harbinger Publications, Inc., Oakland, California

Hall, R. A., & Hinkle, J. E. (1972). Vicarious desensitization of test anxiety. Behavior Research and Therapy, 10, 407-410.

Herbert, S. V. (1984). *A simple hypnotic approach to treat test anxiety in medical students and residents.* Journal of Medication Education, 59(10), 841-842.

Korn, E. R., & Johnson, K. (1983). *Visualization: The uses of imagery in the health professions.* Dow Jones-Irwin, Homewood, Illinois

Levine, M. (1990). *Keeping A Head In School.* Educators Publishing Service, Inc., Cambridge, Massachusetts

Lichstein, K. L. (1988). *Clinical Relaxation Strategies.* John Wiley & Sons, New York.

Nuernberger, P. (1981). *Freedom from Stress: A Holistic Approach.* Himalayan International Institute of Yoga Science and Philosophy of the U.S.A., Honesdale, Pennsylvania.

Millman, J., Bishop, C. H., & Ebel, R. (1965) *Analysis of Test Wiseness.* Educational and Psychological Measurement, 25, 707-726

Rimm, D. C., & Masters, J. C. (1979). *Behavior Therapy, Techniques and Empirical Findings, Second Edition.* Academic Press, Inc., New York, N.Y.

Samuels, M. & Samuels, N. (1975P. *Seeing with the mind's eye: The history, techniques and Uses of Visualization.* Random House, New York, N.Y.

Sapp, M. (1993). Test Anxiety: Applied research, assessment, and treatment interventions. University Press of America, Lanham, Maryland.

Wilson, N. H., & Rotter, J. C. (1986). *Anxiety management training and study skills counseling for students on self esteem and test anxiety and performance.* The School Counselor, 34(1), 18-31.

Order Form

NO MORE TEST ANXIETY (Item 1001) .... $ 17.95
    Includes Audio CD (Item 2001)

Basic Audio CD (Item 2001) .... $ 10.95
    Basic guides for breathing, relaxation,
    auto-hypnosis, and focused studying

Audio Tapes (2) (Item 3001) .... $ 14.95
    Basic guides for breathing, relaxation,
    auto-hypnosis, and focused studying

Audio Tape (Item 3002) .... $ 7.95
    Guides for advanced techniques in relaxation,
    studying, and test-taking skills

Advanced CD (Item 2003) .... $ 10.95
    Advanced techniques in self-hypnosis, and
    The Magic Pen visualization

Audio Tapes (2) (Item 3002) .... $ 14.95
    Advanced techniques in self-hypnosis, and
    The Magic Pen visualization

For fastest service call toll-free **800-362-4777** or FAX order form
below with mc/visa information. When paying by check, please
allow an additional five days before order is shipped.

Learning Skills Publications, LLC
P.O. Box 642442 • Los Angeles, CA 90064-2442
Phone: 800-362-4777 FAX: 310-475-5760

Name _____

Address _____

City, State _____ Zip _____

Item & No. _____Quantity _____ $ _____

Item & No. _____Quantity _____ $ _____

                             Shipping & Handling $ 4.50

❑ Visa   CA Residents add 8.50% Sales Tax $ _____

❑ MC   Total Cost $ _____

Card No. _____ Exp. _____

Signature _____

Order Form

NO MORE TEST ANXIETY (Item 1001) .... $ 17.95
  Includes Audio CD (Item 2001)

Basic Audio CD (Item 2001) .... $ 10.95
  Basic guides for breathing, relaxation,
  auto-hypnosis, and focused studying

Audio Tapes (2) (Item 3001) .... $ 14.95
  Basic guides for breathing, relaxation,
  auto-hypnosis, and focused studying

Audio Tape (Item 3002) .... $ 7.95
  Guides for advanced techniques in relaxation,
  studying, and test-taking skills

Advanced CD (Item 2003) .... $ 10.95
  Advanced techniques in self-hypnosis, and
  The Magic Pen visualization

Audio Tapes (2) (Item 3002) .... $ 14.95
  Advanced techniques in self-hypnosis, and
  The Magic Pen visualization

For fastest service call toll-free **800-362-4777** or FAX order form
below with mc/visa information. When paying by check, please
allow an additional five days before order is shipped.

Learning Skills Publications, LLC
P.O. Box 642442 • Los Angeles, CA 90064-2442
Phone: 800-362-4777 FAX: 310-475-5760

Name _____

Address _____

City, State _____ Zip _____

Item & No. _____Quantity ____ $ _____

Item & No. _____Quantity ____ $ _____

                    Shipping & Handling $ 4.50

❑ Visa   CA Residents add 8.50% Sales Tax $ _____

❑ MC   Total Cost $ _____

Card No. _____ Exp. _____

Signature _____

Order Form

NO MORE TEST ANXIETY (Item 1001) .... $ 17.95
    Includes Audio CD (Item 2001)

Basic Audio CD (Item 2001) .... $ 10.95
    Basic guides for breathing, relaxation,
    auto-hypnosis, and focused studying

Audio Tapes (2) (Item 3001) .... $ 14.95
    Basic guides for breathing, relaxation,
    auto-hypnosis, and focused studying

Audio Tape (Item 3002) .... $ 7.95
    Guides for advanced techniques in relaxation,
    studying, and test-taking skills

Advanced CD (Item 2003) .... $ 10.95
    Advanced techniques in self-hypnosis, and
    The Magic Pen visualization

Audio Tapes (2) (Item 3002) .... $ 14.95
    Advanced techniques in self-hypnosis, and
    The Magic Pen visualization

For fastest service call toll-free **800-362-4777** or FAX order form
below with mc/visa information. When paying by check, please
allow an additional five days before order is shipped.

 Learning Skills Publications, LLC
P.O. Box 642442 • Los Angeles, CA 90064-2442
Phone: 800-362-4777 FAX: 310-475-5760

Name _____

Address _____

City, State _____ Zip _____

Item & No. _____Quantity ____ $ _____

Item & No. _____Quantity ____ $ _____

                        Shipping & Handling $ 4.50

❑ Visa   CA Residents add 8.50% Sales Tax $ _____

❑ MC   Total Cost $ _____

Card No. _____ Exp. _____

Signature _____